THE GHERAṆḌA SAṀHITĀ

A TREATISE ON

HAṬHA YOGA

TRANSLATED BY

S'RĪS' CHANDRA VASU, B.A., F.T.S.

1933

FOREWORD

GHERAṆḌA SAṀHITĀ is a Tāntrika work, treating of Haṭha-Yoga. It consists of a dialogue between the sage Gheraṇḍa and an enquirer called Caṇḍakāpāli. The book is divided into seven Lessons or Chapters and comprises, in all, some three hundred and fifty verses. It closely follows in the foot-steps of the famous treatise on the Haṭha-Yoga, known as Haṭha-Yoga Pradīpikā. In fact, a large number of verses of Gheraṇḍa Saṁhitā correspond *verbatim* with those of the Pradīpikā. It may, therefore, be presumed that one has borrowed from the other, or both have drawn from a common source.

The book teaches Yoga under seven heads or Sādhanas. The first gives directions for the purification of the Body (inside and out). The second relates to Postures, third to Mudrās, the fourth to Pratyāhāra, the fifth to Prāṇāyāma, the sixth to Dhyāna, and the seventh to Samādhi. These are taught successively—a chapter being devoted to each (see Ch. I, 9-10-11).

The theory of Haṭha-Yoga, to put it broadly, is that concentration or Samādhi can be attained by purification of the physical body and certain physical exercises. The relation between physical shell (ghaṭa) and mind is so complete and subtle, and their interaction is so curious and so much enveloped in mystery, that it is not strange that Haṭha-Yogins should have imagined that certain physical training will induce certain mental transformations.

Another explanation—and a later one—is that Haṭha-Yoga means the Yoga or union between ha (ह) and ṭha (ठ); the (ह) meaning the sun; and (ठ) the moon; or the union of the Prāṇa and the Apāna Vāyus. This is also a physical process carried to a higher plane.

The first question, which an unprejudiced enquirer will naturally put, after perusing this book, will be, are all these things possible? and do these practices, produce the result attributed to them?

As to the possibility of these practices, there can be no doubt. They do not violate any anatomical or physiological facts. The practices, some of them at least, may appear revolting and disgusting, but they are not *per se* impossible. Moreover, many of my readers may have come across persons who can practically illustrate these. Such persons are by no means rare in India. Every place of pilgrimage, such as Benares and Allahabad, contains several of them, in various stages of progress. My own Guru showed me and all his visitors at Allahabad and Meerut several of these processes, and taught some people how to do them themselves. The difficult process, such as Vāri-Sāra (Ch. I, 17), Agni-Sāra (I, 20), Daṇḍa-Dhauti (I, 37), Vāso-Dhauti (I, 40), etc., were all shown by him; so also the various Vastis, Neti, Āsanas, etc. Many of these may be classified as gymnastic exercises; their performers need not always be holy or saint-like personages. Several jugglers have been known to perform various Āsanas and Mudrās, and earn their livelihood by showing them to the public. For persons whose muscles have become stiffened and the bones hardened by age, the acquirement of several of these postures, etc., is next to impossible; and it is better that they should not court failure or disappointment by attempting these at an advanced age. But Prāṇāyāma (regulation of breath), Dhāraṇā and Dhyāna are possible for all.

As to the utility of these processes, genuine doubts may be entertained. Many of them may appear puerile, and, if not positively injurious, at least, useless. Although it is not possible within the short space at my command, to give the rationale of *all* these practices, and to justify them to a doubting public, I shall briefly illustrate the advantages of some of them. Thus, to begin with *Vāta-sāra* (I, 15). It is the process of filling the stomach with air, and expelling the wind through the posterior passage. The greatest duct or canal in the human body is the alimentary canal, beginning with the œsophagus (throat) and ending with the rectum. It is some twenty-six feet in length. This great drain contains all the rubbish of the body. Nature periodically cleanses it. Yoga practice makes that cleansing through and voluntary. If the cleansing is incomplete, then the fœtid matters putrify in the stomach and intestines, and generate noxious and deleterious gases which cause diseases. Now *Vāta-sāra* by passing a current of air through the canal, causes the oxidation of the fœtid products of the body; and thus conduces to health, and increases digestion. In fact, it gives a tone to the whole system. Similarly, *Vāri-sāra* is flushing the canal with water instead of air. It thoroughly purges the whole canal; and does the same work as an aperient or a purgative, but with ten times more efficacy and without the injurious effects of these drugs. A person, knowing Vātasāra and Vārisāra, stands in no need of purgatives: the same may be said of Bahiṣkṛta Dhauti (I, 22). By Agnisāra (I, 20), the nerves and muscles of the stomach are brought under the control of volition; and by the gentle shaking of the stomach and the intestines, these organs lose their lethargy, and act with greater vigour. The washing taught in I, 23, 24, is a little dangerous, and may lead to prolapsus, and, a person who can do Vāri-sāra need not do this. The advantages of cleaning the teeth and the tongue are obvious, and, need not be dilated upon. The lengthening of the tongue (I, 32) is necessary for performing hybernation. In doing this, man but imitates the lower creation, like frogs, etc., who in hybernating turn their tongues upward, closing the respiratory passage. Perhaps, the most interesting of all Dhautis is the Vāso-Dhauti (I, 41), which has led unobservant persons to the belief that the Yogins can bring out the intestines by the mouth, wash them, and then swallowing them, again place them in their proper position. This Dhauti is, however, a very simple process, and by so doing the mucus, phlegm, etc., adhering to the sides of the alimentary canal are removed. Water and air could not remove these viscid substances that stick to the sides of the canal.

The Neti, an easy process, clears the nostrils; and cures the tendency or predisposition to cold and catarrh. The Kapālabhāti (I, 55) is a means of cleansing the frontal sinus, said to be the seat of Intelligence. This hollow cannot be directly reached from the outside, but by this process of Kapālabhāti, the nerves surrounding it and spreading over the forehead are brought into play and invigorated.

The various Āsanas taught in Chapter II are gymnastic exercises, good for general health and peace of mind, and calming of passions. The thirty-two Āsanas taught in this book are not all of equal efficacy or importance. Padmāsana is generally approved by all. The others may be practised occasionally for variation and recreation. Some of these postures help in checking animal passions by causing atrophy of the nerves of particular places. Others by straining and stretching of certain muscles create a pleasant sensation of strength and refreshment. The Āsanas are antidotes to the sedentary contemplation of Yoga—a habit which may otherwise lead to mental hallucinations and nervous disorders.

The Mudrās are similar to Āsanas in their action and efficacy. The gazing taught in some of these induces hypnotic sleep; and the Bandhas, by closing all the exits for air, produce a tension within the system, generating thereby a sort of electric current or force, called Kuṇḍalinī S'akti. It is this S'akti which is the help-mate of the Yogins in performing their wonders. The Khecarī Mudrā (III,

25-27) causes levitation of the body. That levitation is possible has now been established beyond doubt. What the particular conditions are under which this takes place, has not yet been fully investigated by Western Science; but that the restraining of breath is one of these conditions may be said to be an undoubted truth. The S'akticālana is a mysterious process, and until a person practically realises it he can hardly believe it. The Mudrās are mixed physical and mental processes, a bridge between Āsanas and Pratyāhāra.

The subject of Pratyāhāra is treated in Chapter IV in five S'lokas. It is the process of restraining the mind from wandering, and restricting it to a fixed idea. All the five senses must be controlled and they should not be allowed to divert the attention.

Prāṇāyāma is the Haṭha-Yoga *par excellence*. It is as dangerous when practised without the supervision of a competent teacher, as it is useful when practised under his supervision. To quote the words of a great authority on this subject: "By practising it according to rule, all diseases are destroyed;

but by doing so irregularly, all diseases are generated, such as hiccough, asthma, cough, headache, ear-ache, diseases of the eye, etc." A practical Guru is absolutely necessary to teach Prāṇāyāma: the directions given in this book are useful as subsidiary rules. Many mistakes and dangers will, however, be warded off by a strict adherence to these rules. The place—a small and solitary cell; the time—spring and autumn; the food—light and sāttvika; these are some of the important preliminaries. Over-exertion, fasting, etc., should be avoided (V, 30). This shows clearly that Haṭha-Yoga is not to be confounded with asceticism. It is far from that. As the training of an athlete is not asceticism, so that of a Haṭha-Yogin is far from being so. True, celibacy is a necessary condition for both, but then that alone does not constitute asceticism. The directions regarding food are peculiar for the people of Bengal, the author of this treatise being apparently a Vaiṣṇava of Bengal. For other countries and persons, these directions may not be applicable in their entirety. But animal food, intoxicating liquors, tobacco, and drugs, are strictly prohibited for all climes.

There are three parts of Prāṇāyāma : Pūraka or drawing in of the breath; Kumbhaka or retaining the breath ; and Recaka or expelling the breath. The proportion of these should be 1: 4: 2, *i.e.*, if Pūraka takes 12 seconds, Kumbhaka should be 48 seconds, and Recaka 24 seconds. The ratio being kept the same, the period of retention, etc., may be increased *ad infinitum.* The beginner should proceed cautiously, should not increase the periods of 16 : 64 : 32 seconds. He should carefully note the various mental and physical changes going on in his system while practising it. Perspiration should be wiped off with a dry towel: nor should he be afraid when he begins to feel a sort of quiver all over the body. Sometimes he may be, jerked off his seat, sometimes he may involuntarily jump about the room like a frog. These should not frighten him. Sometimes there may be no physical manifestations, but mental reactions. He may hear noises, see visions, smell strange odours, or taste delightful delicacies. These are for the most part hallucinations, indicating an excited state of the nervous system. These will soon go off of themselves when not attended to. But flashes of truth will also illumine his heart now and then. Sometimes in the Cidākās'a, he may see reflected distant scenes and events, thoughts of persons will become visible to him; and he himself may leave his body and be carried in space with incalculable velocity. All these symptoms accompany Prāṇāyāma. The Guru must always be near at hand to help and control; for otherwise insanity and not clairvoyance may be the outcome of all this. These are the results of higher stages of Prāṇāyāma. But every person may practise this for two or three minutes, and experience its beneficial results on his own body. Petty disorders, like head-ache, stomach-ache, chill before fever, weariness of body and mind will vanish instantaneously by performing two or three Kumbhakas. Some persons are born with the faculty of performing Prāṇāyāma—Swedenbourg was a living example of this in the West. All persons unconsciously perform Prāṇāyāma when absorbed in deep thinking.

The ten Vāyus (V, 60) are the various nervous forces or currents of the human body. * * *

The various sorts of Kumbhakas taught in Chapter V do not require much elucidation. The Bhrâmarî Kumbhaka (V, 78), however, is a little peculiar. It leads one to hear the various sounds called Anâhata. These sounds are said to be caused within the body by the rushing of the blood through the arteries and veins. The fixing of mind on these sounds soon produces trance.

Dhyâna and Samâdhi are purely mental processes. Fixity and one-pointedness of attention produce trance. The experiments of hypnotism prove this. To fix the mind on one idea produces exaltation of mental faculties.

GHAZIPUR S. C. V.

7th September, 1893

घेरण्डसंहिता ।

THE GHERAṆḌA SAṀHITĀ

प्रथमोपदेशः ।

LESSON FIRST

आदीश्वराय प्रणमामि तस्मै येनोपदिष्टा हठयोगविद्या ।
विराजते प्रोन्नतराजयोगमारोढुमिच्छोरधिरोहिणीव ॥

I salute that Adīs'vara who taught first the science of Haṭha Yoga—a science that stands out as a ladder that leads to the higher heights of Rāja Yoga.

घटस्थयोगकथनम् ।

ON THE TRAINING OF THE PHYSICAL BODY

एकदा चण्डकापालिर्गत्वा घेरण्डकुट्टिरम् ।
प्रणम्य विनयाद् भक्त्या घेरण्डं परिपृच्छति ॥ १ ॥

Once Caṇḍa-Kāpāli went to the hermitage of Gheraṇḍa, saluted him with reverence and devotion, and enquired of him. (1)

श्रीचण्डकापालिरुवाच—

घटस्थयोगं योगेश तत्त्वज्ञानस्य कारणम् ।
इदानीं श्रोतुमिच्छामि योगेश्वर वद प्रभो ॥ २ ॥

CAṆḌA-KĀPĀLI SAID

O Master of Yoga! O best of the Yogins! O Lord! I wish now to hear the physiological Yoga, which leads to the knowledge of truth (or Tattva-jñāna). (2)

घेरण्ड उवाच—

साधु साधु महाबाहो यन्मां त्वं परिपृच्छसि ।
कथयामि हि ते वत्स सावधानोऽवधारय ॥ ३ ॥

GHERAṆḌA REPLIED

Well asked, indeed, O mighty armed! I shall tell thee, O child! what thou askest me. Attend to it with diligence. (3)

नास्ति मायासमः पाशो नास्ति योगात्परं बलम् ।
नास्ति ज्ञानात्परो बन्धुर्नाहंकारात्परो रिपुः ॥ ४ ॥

There are no fetters like those of Illusion (Mâyâ), no strength like that which comes from discipline (Yoga), there is no friend higher than knowledge (Jñâna), and no greater enemy than Egoism (Ahaṁkâra). (4)

अभ्यासात्कादिवर्णानां यथा शास्त्राणि बोधयेत् ।
तथा योगं समासाद्य तत्त्वज्ञानं च लभ्यते ॥ ५ ॥

As by learning the alphabets one can, through practice, master all the sciences, so by thoroughly practising first the (physical) training, one acquires the Knowledge of the True. (5)

सुकृतैर्दुष्कृतैः कार्यैर्जायते प्राणिनां घटः ।
घटादुत्पद्यते कर्म घटीयन्त्रं यथा भ्रमेत् ॥ ६ ॥

On account of good and bad deeds, the bodies of all animated beings are produced, and the bodies give rise to works (Karma which leads to rebirth) and thus the circle is continued like that of a rotating mill. (6)

ऊर्ध्वाधो भ्रमते यद्वद्घटीयन्त्रं गवां वशात् ।
तद्वत्कर्मवशाज्जीवो भ्रमते जन्ममृत्युभिः ॥ ७ ॥

As the rotating mill in drawing water from a well goes up and down, moved by the bullocks (filling and exhausting the buckets again and again), so the soul passes through life and death moved by its Deeds. (7)

आमकुम्भ इवाम्भःस्थो जीर्यमाणः सदा घटः ।
योगानलेन संदह्य घटशुद्धिं समाचरेत् ॥ ८ ॥

Like unto an unbaked earthen pot thrown in water, the body is soon decayed (in this world). Bake it hard in the fire of Yoga in order to strengthen and purify the body. (8)

अथ सप्तसाधनम् ।

शोधनं दृढता चैव स्थैर्यं धैर्यं च लाघवम् ।
प्रत्यक्षं च निर्लिप्तं च घटस्य सप्तसाधनम् ॥ ९ ॥

The seven exercises which appertain to this Yoga of the body are the following: Purificatory, strengthening, steadying, calming, and those leading to lightness, perception, and isolation. (9)

अथ सप्तसाधनलक्षणम् ।

षट्कर्मणा शोधनं च आसनेन भवेद् दृढम् ।
मुद्रया स्थिरता चैव प्रत्याहारेण धीरता ॥ १० ॥

प्राणायामाल्लाघवं च ध्यानात्प्रत्यक्षमात्मनः ।
समाधिना निर्लिप्तं च मुक्तिरेव न संशयः ॥ ११ ॥

1st—The purification is acquired by the regular performance of six practices (to be mentioned shortly); 2nd—Āsana or posture gives Dṛḍhatā or strength; 3rd—Mudrā gives Sthiratā or steadiness; 4th—Pratyāhāra gives Dhīratā or calmness; 5th—Prāṇāyāma gives lightness or Laghiman; 6th—Dhyāna gives perception (Pratyakṣatva) of Self; and 7th—Samādhi gives isolation (Nirliptatā), which is verily the Freedom. (10—11)

अथ शोधनम् ।

धौतिर्वस्तिस्तथा नेतिर्लौलिकी त्राटकं तथा ।
कपालभातिश्चैतानि षट्कर्माणि समाचरेत् ॥ १२ ॥

THE SIX PURIFICATORY PROCESSES

(1) Dhauti; (2) Vasti; (3) Neti; (4) Laulikī; (5) Trāṭaka; (6) Kapālabhāti are the Ṣaṭ-karmas or six practices, known as Sādhana. (12)

PART I

अथ धौतिः ।

अन्तर्धौतिर्दन्तधौतिर्हृद्धौतिर्मूलशोधनम् ।
धौतिं चतुर्विधां कृत्वा घटं कुर्वन्तु निर्मलम् ॥ १३ ॥

THE FOUR INTERNAL DHAUTIS

The Dhautis are of four kinds, and they clear away the impurities of the body. They are: (*a*) Antardhauti (internal washing); (*b*) Dantadhauti (cleaning the teeth); (*c*) Hṛd-dhauti (cleaning the heart); (*d*) Mūlas'odhana (cleaning the rectum). (13)

अथ अन्तर्धौतिः ।

वातसारं वारिसारं वह्निसारं बहिष्कृतम् ।
घटस्य निर्मलार्थाय ह्यन्तर्धौतिश्चतुर्विधा ॥ १४ ॥

(*a*) ANTAR-DHAUTI

Antardhauti is again sub-divided into four parts: Vātasāra (wind purification), Vārisāra (water purification), Vahnisāra (fire purification), and Bahiṣkṛta. (14)

अथ वातसारः ।

काकचञ्चूवदास्येन पिबेद्वायुं शनैः शनैः ।
चालयेदुदरं पश्चाद्वर्त्मना रेचयेच्छनैः ॥ १५ ॥

VĀTASĀRA-DHAUTI

Contract the mouth like the beak of a crow and drink air slowly, and filling the stomach slowly with it, move it therein, and then slowly force it out through the lower passage. (15)

वातसारं परं गोप्यं देहनिर्मलकारणम् ।
सर्वरोगक्षयकरं देहानलविवर्धकम् ॥ १६ ॥

The Vatasâra is a very secret process, it causes the purification of the body, it destroys all diseases and increases the gastric fire. (16)

अथ वारिसारः ।

आकण्ठं पूरयेद्वारि वक्त्रेण च पिबेच्छनैः ।
चालयेदुदरेणैव चोदराद्रेचयेदधः ॥ १७ ॥

VĀRISĀRA-DHAUTI

Fill the mouth with water down to the throat, and then drink it slowly; and then move it through the stomach, forcing it downwards expelling it through the rectum. (17)

वारिसारं परं गोप्यं देहनिर्मलकारकम् ।
साधयेत्तत्प्रयत्नेन देवदेहं प्रपद्यते ॥ १८ ॥

This process should be kept very secret. It purifies the body. And by practising it with care, one gets a luminous or shining body. (18)

वारिसारं परां धौतिं साधयेद्यः प्रयत्नतः ।
मलदेहं शोधयित्वा देवदेहं प्रपद्यते ॥ १९ ॥

The Vārisāra is the highest Dhauti. He who practises it with ease, purifies his filthy body and turns it into a shining one. (19)

अथ अग्निसारः ।

नाभिग्रन्थिं मेरुपृष्ठे शतवारं च कारयेत् ।
अग्निसार इयं धौतिर्योगिनां योगसिद्धिदा ।
उदर्यमामयं त्यक्त्वा जाठराग्निं विवर्धयेत् ॥२०॥

AGNISĀRA OR FIRE PURIFICATION

Press in the naval knot or intestines towards the spine for one hundred times. This is

Agnisâra or fire process. This gives success in the practice of Yoga, it cures all the diseases of the stomach (gastric juice) and increases the internal fire. (20)

एषा धौतिः परा गोप्या देवानामपि दुर्लभा ।
केवलं धौतिमात्रेण देवदेहो भवेद् ध्रुवम् ॥ २१ ॥

This form of Dhauti should be kept very secret, and it is hardly to be attained even by the gods. By this Dhauti alone one certainly gets a luminous body. (21)

अथ बहिष्कृतधौतिः ।

काकीमुद्रां साधयित्वा पूरयेदुदरं मरुत् ।
धारयेदर्धयामं तु चालयेदर्धवर्त्मना ।
एषा धौतिः परा गोप्या न प्रकाश्या कदाचन ॥२२॥

BAHIṢKṚTA-DHAUTI

By Kâkacañcu or crow-bill Mudrâ fill the stomach with air, hold it there for one hour and a half, and then force it down towards the intestines. This Dhauti must be kept a great secret, and must not be revealed to anybody. (22)

अथ प्रक्षालनम् ।

नाभिदघ्ने जले स्थित्वा शक्तिनाडीं विसर्जयेत् ।
कराभ्यां क्षालयेन्नाडीं यावन्मलविसर्जनम् ।
तावत्प्रक्षाल्य नाडीं च उदरे वेशयेत्पुनः ॥ २३ ॥

Then standing in navel-deep water, draw out the S'aktinādī (long intestines), wash the Nādī with hands, so long as its filth is not all washed away; wash it with care, and then draw it in again into the abdomen. (23)

इदं प्रक्षालनं गोप्यं देवानामपि दुर्लभम् ।
केवलं धौतिमात्रेण देवदेहो भवेद् ध्रुवम् ॥ २४ ॥

This process should be kept secret. It is not easily to be attained even by the gods. Simply by this Dhauti one gets Deva-deha (Godlike body). (24)

अथ बहिष्कृतधौतिप्रयोगः ।

यामार्धं धारणां शक्तिं न यावत्साधयेन्नरः ।
बहिष्कृतं महद्धौतिस्तावच्चैव न जायते ॥ २५ ॥

As long as a person has not the power of retaining the breath for an hour and a half (or retaining wind in the stomach for that period), so long he cannot achieve this grand Dhauti or purification, known as Bahiṣkṛtadhauti. (25)

अथ दन्तधौतिः ।

दन्तमूलं जिह्वामूलं रन्ध्रं कर्णयुगस्य च ।
कपालरन्ध्रं पञ्चैते दन्तधौतिं प्रचक्षते ॥ २६ ॥

(*b*) DANTA-DHAUTI, OR TEETH PURIFICATION

Danta-Dhauti is of five kinds: washing of the teeth, of the root of the tongue, of the mouth of each of the two eustachian tubes, and of the frontal sinuses. (26)

अथ दन्तमूलधौतिः ।

खादिरेण रसेनाथ शुद्धमृत्तिकया तथा ।
मार्जयेद्दन्तमूलं च यावत्किल्बिषमाहरेत् ॥ २७ ॥

DANTA-MŪLA-DHAUTI

Rub the teeth with catechu-powder or with pure earth, so long as dental impurities are not removed. (27)

दन्तमूलं परा धौतिर्योगिनां योगसाधने ।
नित्यं कुर्यात्प्रभाते च दन्तरक्षां च योगवित् ।
दन्तमूलं धावनादिकार्येषु योगिनां मतम् ॥ २८ ॥

This teeth-washing is a great Dhauti and an important process in the practice of Yoga for the Yogins. It should be done daily in the morning by the Yogins, in order to preserve the teeth. In purification this is approved of by the Yogins. (28)

अथ जिह्वाशोधनम् ।

अथातः संप्रवक्ष्यामि जिह्वाशोधनकारणम् ।
जरामरणरोगादीन्नाशयेद्दीर्घलम्बिका ॥ २९ ॥

JIHVĀ-S'ODHANA, OR TONGUE-DHAUTI

I shall now tell you the method of cleansing the tongue. The elongation of the tongue destroys old age, death and disease. (29)

अथ जिह्वामूलधौतिप्रयोगः ।

तर्जनीमध्यमानामाख्याङ्गुलित्रययोगतः ।
वेशयेद् गलमध्ये तु मार्जयेल्लम्बिकामलम् ।
शनैः शनैर्मार्जयित्वा कफदोषं निवारयेत् ॥ ३० ॥

Join together the three fingers known as the index, the middle and the ring finger, put them into the throat, and rub well and clean the root of the tongue, and by washing it again throw out the phlegm. (30)

मार्जयेन्नवनीतेन दोहयेच्च पुनः पुनः ।
तदग्रं लौहयन्त्रेण कर्षयित्वा शनैः शनैः ॥ ३१ ॥

Having thus washed it, rub it with butter, and milk it again and again; then by holding the tip of the tongue with an iron instrument pull it out slowly and slowly. (31)

नित्यं कुर्यात्प्रयत्नेन रवेरुदयकेऽस्तके ।
एवं कृते च नित्यं सा लम्बिका दीर्घतां व्रजेत् ॥३२॥

Do this daily with diligence before the rising and setting sun. By so doing the tongue becomes elongated. (32)

अथ कर्णधौतिप्रयोगः ।

तर्जन्यनामिकायोगान्मार्जयेत्कर्णरन्ध्रयोः ।
नित्यमभ्यासयोगेन नादान्तरं प्रकाशयेत् ॥ ३३ ॥

KARṆA-DHAUTI, OR EAR-CLEANING

Clean the two holes of the ears by the index and the ring fingers. By practising it daily, the mystical sounds are heard. (33)

अथ कपालरन्ध्रप्रयोगः ।

वृद्धाङ्गुष्ठेन दक्षेण मार्जयेद्भालरन्ध्रकम् ।
एवमभ्यासयोगेन कफदोषं निवारयेत् ॥ ३४ ॥

KAPĀLA-RANDHRA-DHAUTI

Rub with the thumb of the right hand the depression in the forehead near the bridge of the nose. By the practice of this Yoga, diseases arising from derangements of phlegmatic humours are cured. (34)

नाडी निर्मलतां याति दिव्यदृष्टिः प्रजायते ।
निद्रान्ते भोजनान्ते च दिनान्ते च दिने दिने ॥३५॥

The vessels become purified and clairvoyance is induced. This should be practised daily after awakening from sleep, after meals, and in the evening. (35)

अथ हृद्धौतिः ।

हृद्धौतिं त्रिविधां कुर्याद्दण्डवमनवाससा ॥ ३६ ॥

(c) HṚD-DHAUTI

Hṛd-Dhauti, or purification of the heart (or rather the throat) is of three kinds, *viz.*, by a Daṇḍa (a stick), Vamana (vomiting), and by Vāsas (cloth) (36)

रम्भादण्डं हरिद्दण्डं वेत्रदण्डं तथैव च ।
हृन्मध्ये चालयित्वा तु पुनः प्रत्याहरेच्छनैः ॥ ३७ ॥

DAṆḌA-DHAUTI

Take either a plantain stalk or a stalk of turmeric (Haridrā) or a stalk of cane, and thrust it slowly into the gullet and then draw it out slowly. (37)

कफं पित्तं तथा क्लेदं रेचयेदूर्ध्ववर्त्मना ।
दण्डधौतिविधानेन हृद्रोगं नाशयेद् ध्रुवम् ॥ ३८ ॥

By this process all the phlegm, bile and other impurities are expelled out of the mouth. By this Daṇḍa-Dhauti every kind of heart-disease is surely cured. (38)

अथ वमनधौतिः ।

भोजनान्ते पिबेद्वारि चाकण्ठं पूरितं सुधीः ।
उर्ध्वां दृष्टिं क्षणं कृत्वा तज्जलं वमयेत्पुनः ।
नित्यमभ्यासयोगेन कफपित्तं निवारयेत् ॥ ३९ ॥

VAMANA-DHAUTI

After meal, let the wise practitioner drink water full up to the throat, then looking for a short while upwards, let him vomit it out again. By daily practising this Yoga, disorders of the phlegm and bile are cured. (39)

अथ वासोधौतिः ।

चतुरङ्गुलविस्तारं सूक्ष्मवस्त्रं शनैर्ग्रसेत् ।
पुनः प्रत्याहरेदेतत्प्रोच्यते धौतिकर्मकम् ॥ ४० ॥

VĀSO-DHAUTI

Let him swallow slowly a thin cloth, four fingers wide, then let him draw it out again. This is called Vāso-Dhauti. (40)

गुल्मज्वरप्लीहाकुष्ठकफपित्तं विनश्यति ।
आरोग्यं बलपुष्टिश्च भवेत्तस्य दिने दिने ॥ ४१ ॥

This cures Gulma or abdominal diseases, fever, enlarged spleen, leprosy, and other skin diseases and disorders of phlegm and bile, and day by day the practitioner gets health, strength, and cheerfulness. (41)

अथ मूलशोधनम् ।

अपानक्रूरता तावद्यावन्मूलं न शोधयेत् ।
तस्मात्सर्वप्रयत्नेन मूलशोधनमाचरेत् ॥ ४२ ॥

(d) MŪLA-S'ODHANA, OR PURIFICATION OF THE RECTUM

The Apânavâyu does not flow freely so long as the rectum is not purified. Therefore with the greatest care let him practise this purification of the large intestines. (42)

पित्तमूलस्य दण्डेन मध्यमाङ्गुलिनाऽपि वा ।
यत्नेन क्षालयेद् गुह्यं वारिणा च पुनः पुनः ॥ ४३ ॥

By the stalk of the root of Haridrâ (turmeric) or the middle finger, the rectum should be carefully cleansed with water over and over again. (43)

वारयेत्कोष्ठकाठिन्यमामजीर्णं निवारयेत् ।
कारणं कान्तिपुष्ट्योश्च वह्निमण्डलदीपनम् ॥ ४४ ॥

This destroys constipation, indigestion, and dyspepsia, and increases the beauty and vigour of the body and enkindles the sphere of the fire (*i.e.*, the gastric juice). (44)

End of Dhautis

PART II

अथ वस्तिप्रकरणम् ।

जलवस्तिः शुष्कवस्तिर्वस्तिः स्याद् द्विविधा स्मृता ।
जलवस्तिं जले कुर्याच्छुष्कवस्तिं सदा क्षितौ ॥ ४५ ॥

VASTIS

The Vastis described are of two kinds, *viz.*: Jala Vasti (or water Vasti) and Śuṣka Vasti (or dry Vasti). Water Vasti is done in water and dry Vasti always on land. (45)

अथ जलवस्तिः ।

नाभिदघ्ने जले पायुं न्यस्तवानुत्कटासनम् ।
आकुञ्चनं प्रसारं च जलवस्तिं समाचरेत् ॥ ४६ ॥

JALA-VASTI

Entering water up to the navel and assuming the posture called Utkaṭāsana, let him contract and dilate the sphincter-muscle of the anus. This is called Jala-Vasti. (46)

प्रमेहं च उदावर्तं क्रूरवायुं निवारयेत् ।
भवेत्स्वच्छन्ददेहश्च कामदेवसमो भवेत् ॥ ४७ ॥

This cures Prameha (urinary disorders), udāvarta (disorders of digestion) and Krūravāyu (disorders of the wind). The body becomes free from all diseases and becomes as beautiful as that of the god Cupid. (47)

अथ स्थलवस्तिः ।

पश्चिमोत्तानतो वस्तिं चालयित्वा शनैरधः ।
अश्विनीमुद्रया पायुमाकुञ्चयेत् प्रसारयेत् ॥ ४८ ॥

STHALA-VASTI

Assuming the posture called Pas'cimottāna, let him move the intestines slowly downwards, then contract and dilate the sphincter-muscle of the anus with As'vinī-Mudrā. (48)

एवमभ्यासयोगेन कोष्ठदोषो न विद्यते ।
विवर्धयेज्जाठराग्निमामवातं विनाशयेत् ॥ ४९ ॥

By this practice of Yoga, constipation never occurs, and it increases gastric fire and cures flatulence. (49)

End of Vasti-Karma

PART III

अथ नेतियोगः ।

वितस्तिमानं सूक्ष्मसूत्रं नासानाले प्रवेशयेत् ।
मुखान्निर्गमयेत्पश्चात् प्रोच्यते नेतिकर्मकम् ॥ ५० ॥

NETI

Take a thin thread, measuring half a cubit, and insert it into the nostrils, and passing it through, pull it out by the mouth. This is called Neti-Kriyā. (50)

साधनान्नेतिकार्यस्य खेचरीसिद्धिमाप्नुयात् ।
कफदोषा विनश्यन्ति दिव्यदृष्टिः प्रजायते ॥ ५१ ॥

By practising the Neti-Kriyā, one obtains Khecarī Siddhi. It destroys the disorders of phlegm and produces clairvoyance or clear sight. (51)

PART IV

अथ लौलिकीयोगः ।

अमन्दवेगेन तुन्दं भ्रामयेत्पार्श्वयोर्द्वयोः ।
सर्वरोगान्निहन्तीह देहानलविवर्धनम् ॥ ५२ ॥

LAULIKĪ-YOGA

With great force move the stomach and intestines from one side to the other. This is called Laulikī-Yoga. This destroys all diseases and increases the bodily fire. (52)

PART V

अथ त्राटकम् ।

निमेषोन्मेषकं त्यक्त्वा सूक्ष्मलक्ष्यं निरीक्षयेत् ।
पतन्ति यावदश्रूणि त्राटकं प्रोच्यते बुधैः ॥ ५३ ॥

TRĀṬAKA OR GAZING

Gaze steadily without winking at any small object, until tears begin to flow. This is called Trāṭaka by the wise. (53)

एवमभ्यासयोगेन शांभवी जायते ध्रुवम् ।
नेत्ररोगा विनश्यन्ति दिव्यदृष्टिः प्रजायते ॥ ५४ ॥

By practising this Yoga, S'āṃbhavī Mudrā is obtained; and certainly all diseases of the eye are destroyed and clairvoyance is induced. (54)

PART VI

अथ कपालभातिः ।

वामक्रमेण व्युत्क्रमेण शीत्क्रमेण विशेषतः ।
भालभातिं त्रिधा कुर्यात्कफदेषं निवारयेत् ॥ ५५ ॥

KAPĀLABHĀTI

The Kapâlabhâti is of three kinds: Vâma-krama, Vyut-krama, and S'ît-krama. They destroy disorders of phlegm. (55)

अथ वामक्रमकपालभातिः ।

इडया पूरयेद्वायुं रेचयेत्पिङ्गलया पुनः ।
पिङ्गलया पूरयित्वा पुनश्चन्द्रेण रेचयेत् ॥ ५६ ॥

VĀMA-KRAMA

Draw the wind through the left nostril and expel it through the right, and draw it again through the right and expel it through the left. (56)

पूरकं रेचकं कृत्वा वेगेन न तु चालयेत् ।
एवमभ्यासयोगेन कफदोषं निवारयेत् ॥ ५७ ॥

This inspiration and expiration must be done without any force. This practice destroys disorders due to phlegm. (57)

अथ व्युत्क्रमकपालभातिः ।

नासाभ्यां जलमाकृष्य पुनर्वक्त्रेण रेचयेत् ।
पायं पायं व्युत्क्रमेण श्लेष्मदोषं निवारयेत् ॥ ५८ ॥

VYUT-KRAMA

Draw the water through the two nostrils and expel it through the mouth slowly and slowly. This is called Vyut-krama which destroys disorders due to phlegm. (58)

अथ शीत्क्रमकपालभातिः ।

शीत्कृत्य पीत्वा वक्त्रेण नासानालैर्विरेचयेत् ।
एवमभ्यासयोगेन कामदेवसमो भवेत् ॥ ५९ ॥

SĪT-KRAMA

Suck water through the mouth and expel it through the nostrils. By this practice of Yoga one becomes like the god Cupid. (59)

न जायते वार्द्धकं च ज्वरो नैव प्रजायते ।
भवेत्स्वच्छन्ददेहश्च कफदोषं निवारयेत् ॥ ६० ॥

इति श्रीघेरण्डसंहितायां घेरण्डचण्डसंवादे षट्कर्म-
साधनं नाम प्रथमोपदेशः समाप्तः ।

Old age never comes to him and decrepitude never disfigures him. The body becomes healthy, elastic, and disorders due to phlegm are destroyed. (60)

End of the first lesson

द्वितीयोपदेशः ।

LESSON THE SECOND

अथ आसनानि ।

घेरण्ड उवाच—

आसनानि समस्तानि यावन्तो जीवजन्तवः ।
चतुरशीतिलक्षाणि शिवेन कथितानि च ॥ १ ॥

THE ĀSANAS OR POSTURES

GHERAṆḌA SAID

There are eighty-four hundreds of thousands of Āsanas described by Śiva. The postures are as many in number as there are numbers of species of living creatures in this universe. (1)

तेषां मध्ये विशिष्टानि षोडशोनं शतं कृतम् ।
तेषां मध्ये मर्त्यलोके द्वात्रिंशदासनं शुभम् ॥ २ ॥

Among them eighty-four are the best; and among these eighty-four, thirty-two have been found useful for mankind in this world. (2)

अथ आसनानां भेदाः ।

सिद्धं पद्मं तथा भद्रं मुक्तं वज्रं च स्वस्तिकम् ।
सिंहं च गोमुखं वीरं धनुरासनमेव च ॥ ३ ॥
मृतं गुप्तं तथा मात्स्यं मत्स्येन्द्रासनमेव च ।
गोरक्षं पश्चिमोत्तानमुत्कटं संकटं तथा ॥ ४ ॥
मयूरं कुक्कुटं कूर्मं तथा चोत्तानकूर्मकम् ।
उत्तानमण्डुकं वृक्षं मण्डुकं गरुडं वृषम् ॥ ५ ॥
शलभं मकरं चोष्ट्रं भुजङ्गं योगमासनम् ।
द्वात्रिंशदासनानां तु मर्त्यलोके हि सिद्धिदा ॥ ६ ॥

DIFFERENT KINDS OF POSTURES

The thirty-two Āsanas that give perfection in this mortal world are the following:

(1) Siddha (*Perfect posture*); (2) Padma (*Lotus posture*); (3) Bhadra (*Gentle posture*); (4) Mukta (*Free posture*); (5) Vajra (*Thunderbolt posture*); (6) Svastika (*Prosperous posture*); (7) Siṃha (*Lion posture*); (8) Gomukha (*Cow-mouth posture*); (9) Vīra (*Heroic posture*);

(10) Dhanus (*Bow posture*); (11) Mṛta (*Corpse posture*); (12) Gupta (*Hidden posture*); (13) Mātṣya (*Fish posture*); (14) Matsyendra; (15) Gorakṣa; (16) Pas'cimottāna; (17) Utkaṭa (*Hazardous posture*); (18) Saṃkaṭa (*Dangerous posture*); (19) Mayūra (*Peacock posture*); (20) Kukkuṭa (*Cock posture*); (21) Kūrma (*Tortoise posture*); (22) Uttana Kūrmaka; (23) Uttāna Maṇḍuka; (24) Vṛkṣa (*Tree posture*); (25) Maṇḍuka (*Frog posture*); (26) Garuḍa (*Eagle posture*); (27) Vṛṣa (*Bull posture*); (28) S'alabha (*Locust posture*); (29) Makara (*Dolphin posture*); (30) Uṣṭra (*Camel posture*); (31) Bhujaṅga (*Snake posture*); (32) Yoga. (3—6)

अथ आसनानां प्रयोगाः ।

अथ सिद्धासनम् ।

योनिस्थानकमङ्घ्रिमूलघटितं संपीड्य गुल्फेतरं
मेढ्रोपर्यथ संनिधाय चिबुकं कृत्वा हृदि स्थापितम् ।
स्थाणुः संयमितेन्द्रियोऽचलदृशा पश्यन्भ्रुवोरन्तरं
ह्येतन्मोक्षकवाटभेदनकरं सिद्धासनं प्रोच्यते ॥ ७ ॥

(1) THE SIDDHĀSANA

The practitioner who has subdued his passions, having placed one heel at the anal aperture should keep the other heel on the root of the generative organ; afterwards he should rest his chin upon the chest, and being quiet and straight, gaze at the spot between the two eye-brows. This is called the Siddhāsana which leads to emancipation. (7)

अथ पद्मासनम् ।

वामोरूपरि दक्षिणं हि चरणं संस्थाप्य वामं तथा
दक्षोरूपरि पश्चिमेन विधिना कृत्वा कराभ्यां दृढम् ।
अङ्गुष्ठौ हृदये निधाय चिबुकं नासाग्रमालोकये-
त्सर्वव्याधिविनाशनक्षममिदं पद्मासनं प्रोच्यते ॥८॥

(2) THE PADMĀSANA

Place the right foot on the left thigh and similarly the left one on the right thigh, also cross the hands behind the back and firmly catch hold of the great toes of feet so crossed. Place the chin on the chest and fix the gaze on the tip of the nose. This posture is called the Padmâsana (or Lotus posture). This posture destroys all diseases. (8)

अथ भद्रासनम् ।

गुल्फौ च वृषणस्याधो व्युत्क्रमेण समाहितः ।
पादाङ्गुष्ठौ कराभ्यां च धृत्वा वै पृष्ठदेशतः ॥ ९ ॥
जालन्धरं समासाद्य नासाग्रमवलोकयेत् ।
भद्रासनं भवेदेतत्सर्वव्याधिविनाशकम् ॥ १० ॥

(3) THE BHADRĀSANA

Place the heels crosswise under the testes attentively; cross the hands behind the back and take hold of the toes of the feet. Fix the gaze on the tip of the nose, having previously adopted the Mudrâ called Jâlandhara. This is the Bhadrâsana (or happy posture) which destroys all sorts of diseases. (9—10)

अथ मुक्तासनम् ।

पायुमूले वामगुल्फं दक्षगुल्फं तथोपरि ।
समकायशिरोग्रीवं मुक्तासनं तु सिद्धिदम् ॥ ११ ॥

(4) THE MUKTĀSANA

Place the left heel at the root of the organ of generation and the right heel above that, keep the head and the neck straight with the body. This posture is called the Muktāsana. It gives Siddhi (perfection). (11)

अथ वज्रासनम् ।

जङ्घाभ्यां वज्रवत्कृत्वा गुदपार्श्वे पदावुभौ ।
वज्रासनं भवेदेतद्योगिनां सिद्धिदायकम् ॥ १२ ॥

(5) THE VAJRĀYUDHĀSANA

Make the thighs tight like vajra and place the legs by the two sides of the anus. This is called the Vajrāsana. It gives psychic powers to the Yogin. (12)

अथ स्वस्तिकासनम् ।

जानूर्वोरन्तरे कृत्वा योगी पादतले उभे ।
ऋजुकाय: समासीत स्वस्तिकं तत्प्रचक्षते ॥ १३ ॥

(6) THE SVASTIKĀSANA

Drawing the legs and thighs together and placing the feet between them, keeping the body in its easy condition and sitting straight, constitute the posture called the Svastikāsana. (13)

अथ सिंहासनम् ।

गुल्फौ च वृषणस्याधो व्युत्क्रमेणोर्ध्वतां गतौ ।
चितियुग्मं भूमिसंस्थं हस्तौ कृत्वा च जानुनोः ॥१४॥
व्यात्तवक्त्रो जलन्ध्रेण नासाग्रमवलोकयेत् ।
सिंहासनं भवेदेतत्सर्वव्याधिविनाशकम् ॥ १५ ॥

(7) The Siṃhāsana

The two heels to be placed under the scrotum contrariwise (*i.e.*, left heel on the right side and the right heel on the left side of it) and turned upwards, the knees to be placed on the ground, and the hands placed on the knees, mouth to be kept open; practising the Jālandhara mudrā one should fix his gaze on the tip of the nose. This is the Siṃhāsana (Lion-posture), the destroyer of all diseases. (14—15)

अथ गोमुखासनम् ।

पादौ च भूमौ संस्थाप्य पृष्ठपार्श्वे निवेशयेत् ।
स्थिरं कायं समासाद्य गोमुखं गोमुखाकृति ॥ १६ ॥

(8) The Gomukhāsana

The two feet to be placed on the ground, and the heels to be placed contrariwise under the buttocks; the body to be kept steady and the mouth raised, and sitting equably: this is called the Gomukhâsana: resembling the mouth of a cow. (16)

अथ वीरासनम् ।

एकं पादमथैकस्मिन्विन्यसेदूरुसंस्थितम् ।
इतरस्मिंस्तथा पश्चाद्वीरासनमितीरितम् ॥ १७ ॥

(9) THE VĪRĀSANA

One leg (the right foot) to be placed on the other (left) thigh, and the other foot to be turned backwards. This is called the Vīrâsana (Hero-posture). (17)

अथ धनुरासनम् ।

प्रसार्य पादौ भुवि दण्डरूपौ करद्वयात्ताङ्गुलिपादयुग्मम् ।
कृत्वा धनुर्वत्परिवर्तिताङ्गं निगद्यते वै धनुरासनं तत् ॥ १८ ॥

(10) THE DHANURĀSANA

Stretching the legs on the ground like a stick, and catching hold of (the toes of) the feet with the hands, and making the body like a bow, is called the Dhanurâsana or Bow posture. (18)

अथ मृतासनम् ।

उत्तानं शववद् भूमौ शयनं तु शवासनम् ।
शवासनं श्रमहरं चित्तविश्रान्तिकारणम् ॥ १९ ॥

(11) THE MṚTĀSANA

Lying flat on the ground (on one's back) like a corpse is called the Mṛtâsana (the Corpse-posture). This posture destroys fatigue, and quiets the agitation of the mind. (19)

अथ गुप्तासनम् ।

जानूर्वोरन्तरे पादौ कृत्वा पादौ च गोपयेत् ।
पदोपरि च संस्थाप्य गुदं गुप्तासनं विदुः ॥ २० ॥

(12) THE GUPTĀSANA

Hide the two feet between the knees and thighs, and place the anus on the feet. This is known as the Guptâsana (Hidden-posture). (20)

अथ मत्स्यासनम् ।

मुक्तपद्मासनं कृत्वा ह्युत्तानशयनं चरेत् ।
कूर्पराभ्यां शिरो वेष्ट्यं रोगघ्नं मात्स्यमासनम् ॥ २१ ॥

(13) THE MATSYĀSANA

Make the Padmâsana-posture (as stated in verse 8) without the crossing of the arms; lie on the back, holding the head by the two elbows. This is the Matsyâsana (Fish-posture), the destroyer of diseases. (21)

अथ मत्स्येन्द्रासनम् ।

उदरं पश्चिमाभासं कृत्वा तिष्ठत्ययत्नतः ।
नम्रितं वामपादं हि दक्षजानूपरि न्यसेत् ॥ २२ ॥
तत्र याम्यं कूर्परं च वक्त्रं याम्यकरेऽपि च ।
भ्रुवोर्मध्ये गता दृष्टिः पीठं मात्स्येन्द्रमुच्यते ॥ २३ ॥

(14) THE MATSYENDRĀSANA

Keeping the abdominal region at ease like the back, bending the left leg, place it on the right thigh; then place on this the elbow of the right hand, and place the face on the palm of the right hand and fix the gaze between the eye-brows. This is called the Mâtsyendra posture. (22—23)

अथ गोरक्षासनम् ।

जानूर्वोरन्तरे पादावुत्तानौ व्यक्तसंस्थितौ ।
गुल्फौ चाच्छाद्य हस्ताभ्यामुत्तानाभ्यां प्रयत्नतः ॥२४॥

कण्ठसंकोचनं कृत्वा नासाग्रमवलोकयेत् ।
गोरक्षासनमित्याह योगिनां सिद्धिकारणम् ॥ २५ ॥

(15) THE GORAKṢĀSANA

Between the knees and the thighs, the two feet turned upward and placed in a hidden way, the heels being carefully covered by the two hands outstretched; the throat being contracted, let one fix the gaze on the tip of the nose. This is called the Gorakṣâsana. It gives success to the Yogins. (24—25)

अथ पश्चिमोत्तानासनम् ।

प्रसार्य पादौ भुवि दण्डरूपौ विन्यस्तभालं चितियुग्ममध्ये ।
यत्नेन पादौ च धृतौ कराभ्यां तत्पश्चिमोत्तानमिहासनं स्यात् ॥

(16) THE PAS'CIMOTTĀNĀSANA

Stretch the two legs on the ground, stiff like a stick (the heels not touching), and place the forehead on the two knees, and catch with the hands the toes. This is called the Pas'cimottânâsana. (26)

अथ उत्कटासनम् ।

अङ्गुष्ठाभ्यामवष्टभ्य धरां गुल्फौ च खे गतौ ।
तत्रोपरि गुदं न्यस्य विज्ञेयं तूत्कटासनम् ॥ २७ ॥

(17) THE UTKAṬĀSANA

Let the toes touch the ground, and the heels be raised in the air; place the anus on the heels: this is known as the Utkaṭāsana. (27)

अथ संकटासनम् ।

वामपादं चितेर्मूलं विन्यस्य धरणीतले ।
पाददण्डेन याम्येन वेष्टयेद्वामपादकम् ।
जानुयुग्मे करयुगमेतत्संकटमासनम् ॥ २८ ॥

(18) THE SAṄKAṬĀSANA

Placing the left foot and the leg on the ground, surround the left foot by the right leg; and place the two hands on the two knees. This is the Saṅkaṭāsana. (28)

अथ मयूरासनम् ।

पाण्योस्तलाभ्यामवलम्ब्य भूमिं तत्कूर्परस्थापितनाभिपार्श्वम् ।
उच्चासनो दण्डवदुत्थितः खे मायूरमेतत्प्रवदन्ति पीठम् ॥२९॥
बहु कदशनभुक्तं भस्म कुर्यादशेषं
जनयति जठराग्निं जारयेत्कालकूटम् ।
हरति सकलरोगानाशु गुल्मज्वरादी-
न्भवति विगतदोषं ह्यासनं श्रीमयूरम् ॥ ३० ॥

(19) The Mayūrāsana

Place the palms of the two hands on the ground, place the umbilical region on the two elbows, stand upon the hands, the legs being raised in the air, and crossed like Padmâsana. This is called the Mayûrâsana (Peacock-Posture). The Peacock-Posture destroys the effects of unwholesome food; it produces heat in the stomach; it destroys the effects of deadly poisons; it easily cures diseases, like Gulma and fever; such is this useful posture. (29—30)

अथ कुक्कुटासनम् ।

पद्मासनं समासाद्य जानूर्वोरन्तरे करौ ।
कूर्पराभ्यां समासीन उच्चस्थः कुक्कुटासनम् ॥ ३१ ॥

(20) The Kukkuṭāsana

Sitting on the ground, cross the legs in the Padmâsana posture, thrust down the hands between the thighs and the knees, stand on the hands, supporting the body on the elbows. This is called the Cock-Posture. (31)

अथ कूर्मासनम् ।

गुल्फौ च वृषणस्याधो व्युत्क्रमेण समाहितौ ।
ऋजुकायशिरोग्रीवं कूर्मासनमितीरितम् ॥ ३२ ॥

(21) THE KŪRMĀSANA

Place the heels contrariwise under the scrotum, stiffen (or keep at ease) the head, neck and body. This is called the Tortoise-Posture. (32)

अथ उत्तानकूर्मकासनम् ।

कुक्कुटासनबन्धस्थं कराभ्यां धृतकन्धरम् ।
पीठं कूर्मवदुत्तानमेतदुत्तानकूर्मकम् ॥ ३३ ॥

(22) THE UTTĀNAKŪRMAKĀSANA

Assume the Cock-posture (as stated in verse 31), catch hold of the neck with the hands, and stand stretched like a tortoise. This is the Uttānakūrmakāsana. (33)

अथ मण्डुकासनम् ।

पृष्ठदेशे पादतलावङ्गुष्ठौ द्वौ च संस्पृशेत् ।
जानुयुग्मं पुरस्कृत्य साधयेन्मण्डुकासनम् ॥ ३४ ॥

(23) THE MAṆḌUKĀSANA

Carry the feet towards the back, the toes touching each other, and place the knees forwards. This is called the Frog-posture. (34)

अथ उत्तानमण्डुकासनम् ।

मण्डुकासनमध्यस्थं कूर्पराभ्यां धृतं शिरः ।
एतद् भेकवदुत्तानमेतदुत्तानमण्डुकम् ॥ ३५ ॥

(24) THE UTTĀNAMAṆḌUKĀSANA

Assume the frog-posture (as in verse 34), hold the head by the elbows, and stand up like a frog. This is called the Uttānamaṇḍukāsana. (35)

अथ वृक्षासनम् ।

वामोरुमूलदेशे च याम्यं पादं निधाय वै ।
तिष्ठेत्तु वृक्षवद्भूमौ वृक्षासनमिदं विदुः ॥ ३६ ॥

(25) THE VṚKṢĀSANA

Stand straight on one leg (the left), bending the right leg, and placing the right foot on the root of the left thigh; standing thus like a tree on the ground, is called the Tree-posture. (36)

अथ गरुडासनम् ।

जङ्घोरुभ्यां धरां पीड्य स्थिरकायो द्विजानुना ।
जानूपरि करद्वन्द्वं गरुडासनमुच्यते ॥ ३७ ॥

(26) THE GARUḌĀSANA

Place the legs and the thighs on the ground pressing it, steady the body with the two knees, place the two hands on the knees: this is called the Garuḍa-posture. (37)

अथ वृषासनम् ।

याम्यगुल्फे पायुमूलं वामभागे पदेतरम् ।
विपरीतं स्पृशेद्भूमिं वृषासनमिदं भवेत् ॥ ३८ ॥

(27) THE VṚṢĀSANA

Place the anus on the right heel, on the left of it place the left leg crossing it opposite way, and touch the ground. This is called the Bull-posture. (38)

अथ शलभासनम् ।

अध्यास्य शेते करयुग्मवक्षा आलम्ब्य भूमिं करयोस्तलाभ्याम् ।
पादौ च शून्ये च वितस्ति चोर्ध्वं वदन्ति पीठं शलभं मुनीन्द्राः ॥

(28) THE S'ALABHĀSANA

Lie on the ground face downwards, the two hands being placed on the chest, touching the ground with the palms, raise the legs in the air one cubit high. This is called the Locust-posture. (39)

अथ मकरासनम् ।

अध्यास्य शेते हृदयं निधाय भूमौ च पादौ प्रविसार्यमाणौ ।
शिरश्च धृत्वा करदण्डयुग्मे देहाग्निकारं मकरासनं तत् ॥ ४० ॥

(29) THE MAKARĀSANA

Lie on the ground face downwards, the chest touching the earth, the two legs being stretched: catch the head with the two arms. This is Makarāsana, the increaser of the bodily heat. (40)

अथ उष्ट्रासनम् ।

अध्यास्य शेते पदयुग्मव्यस्तं पृष्ठे निधायापि धृतं कराभ्याम् ।
आकुञ्चय सम्यग्घ्युदरास्यगाढमौष्ट्रं च पीठं यतयो वदन्ति ॥

(30) THE UṢṬRĀSANA

Lie on the ground face downwards, turn up the legs and place them towards the back, catch the legs with the hands, contract forcibly the mouth and the abdomen. This is called the Camel-posture. (41)

अथ भुजङ्गासनम् ।

अङ्गुष्ठनाभिपर्यन्तमधोभूमौ विनिन्यसेत् ।
धरां करतलाभ्यां धृत्वोर्ध्वशीर्षः फणीव हि ॥ ४२ ॥
देहाग्निर्वर्धते नित्यं सर्वरोगविनाशनम् ।
जागर्ति भुजगी देवी भुजङ्गासनसाधनात् ॥ ४३ ॥

(31) THE BHUJAṄGĀSANA

Let the body, from the navel downwards to the toes, touch the ground, place the palms on the ground, raise the head (the upper portion of the body) like a serpent. This is called the Serpent-posture. This always increases the bodily heat, destroys all diseases, and by the practice of this posture the serpent-goddess (the kuṇḍalinī force) awakes. (42—43)

अथ योगासनम् ।

उत्तानौ चरणौ कृत्वा संस्थाप्योपरि जानुनोः ।
आसनोपरि संस्थाप्य चोत्तानं करयुग्मकम् ॥ ४४ ॥

पूरकैर्वायुमाकृष्य नासाग्रमवलोकयेत् ।
योगासनं भवेदेतद्योगिनां योगसाधने ॥ ४५ ॥

इति श्रीघेरण्डसंहितायां घेरण्डचण्डसंवादे आसनप्रयोगो नाम
द्वितीयोपदेशः समाप्तः ।

(32) THE YOGĀSANA

Turn the feet upwards, place them on the knees; then place the hands on the ground with the palms turned upwards; inspire, and fix the gaze on the tip of the nose. This is called the Yoga-posture assumed by the Yogins when practising Yoga. (44—45)

End of the second lesson

तृतीयोपदेशः ।

LESSON THE THIRD

अथ मुद्राकथनम् ।

घेरण्ड उवाच—

महामुद्रा नभोमुद्रा उड्डीयानं जलन्धरम् ।
मूलबन्धो महाबन्धो महावेधश्च खेचरी ॥ १ ॥
विपरीतकरी योनिर्वज्रोली शक्तिचालनी ।
ताडागी माण्डुकी मुद्रा शांभवी पञ्चधारणा ॥ २ ॥
अश्विनी पाशिनी काकी मातङ्गी च भुजङ्गिनी ।
पञ्चविंशतिमुद्राश्च सिद्धिदा इह योगिनाम् ॥ ३ ॥

ON MUDRĀS

GHERAṆḌA SAID

There are twenty-five mudrās, the practice of which gives success to the Yogins. They are:

(1) Mahā-mudrā, (2) Nabho-mudrā, (3) Uḍḍīyāna, (4) Jālandhara, (5) Mūlabandha, (6) Mahābandha, (7) Mahāvedha, (8) Khecarī, (9) Viparītakaraṇī, (10) Yoni, (11) Vajrolī, (12) Śakticālanī, (13) Tāḍāgī, (14) Māṇḍukī, (15) Śāṁbhavī, (16) Pañcadhāraṇā (five dhāraṇās), (21) Aśvinī, (22) Pāśinī, (23) Kākī, (24) Mātaṅgī, and (25) Bhujaṅginī. (1—3)

अथ मुद्राणां फलकथनम् ।

मुद्राणां पटलं देवि कथितं तव संनिधौ ।
येन विज्ञातमात्रेण सर्वसिद्धिः प्रजायते ॥ ४ ॥
गोपनीयं प्रयत्नेन न देयं यस्य कस्यचित् ।
प्रीतिदं योगिनां चैव दुर्लभं मरुतामपि ॥ ५ ॥

THE ADVANTAGES OF PRACTISING MUDRĀS

Maheśvara, when addressing his consort, has recited the advantages of Mudrās in these words: "O Devi! I have told you all the Mudrās; their knowledge leads to adeptship. It should be kept secret with great care, and should not be taught indiscriminately to every one. This gives happiness to the Yogins, and is not to be easily attained by the maruts (gods of air) even." (4—5)

अथ महामुद्राकथनम् ।

पायुमूलं वामगुल्फे संपीड्य दृढयत्नतः ।
याम्यपादं प्रसार्याथ करोपात्तपदाङ्गुलिः ॥ ६ ॥
कण्ठसंकोचनं कृत्वा भ्रुवोर्मध्यं निरीक्षयेत् ।
महामुद्राभिधा मुद्रा कथ्यते चैव सूरिभिः ॥ ७ ॥

(1) MAHĀ-MUDRĀ

Pressing carefully the anus by the left heel, stretch the right leg, and take hold of the toes by the hands; contract the throat (not exhaling), and fix the gaze between the eye-brows. This is called Mahā-mudrā by the wise. (6—7)

अथ महामुद्राफलकथनम् ।

क्षयकासगुदावर्तप्लीहाजीर्णज्वरं तथा ।
नाशयेत्सर्वरोगांश्च महामुद्रा च साधनात् ॥ ८ ॥

Its benefits

The practice of Mahā-mudrā cures consumption, the obstruction of the bowels, the enlargement of the spleen, indigestion and fever—in fact it cures all diseases. (8)

अथ नभोमुद्राकथनम् ।

यत्र यत्र स्थितो योगी सर्वकार्येषु सर्वदा ।
ऊर्ध्वजिह्वः स्थिरो भूत्वा धारयेत्पवनं सदा ।
नभोमुद्रा भवेदेषा योगिनां रोगनाशिनी ॥ ९ ॥

(2) NABHO-MUDRĀ

In whatever business a Yogin may be engaged, wherever he may be, let him always keep his tongue turned upwards (towards the soft palate), and restrain the breath. This is called Nabho-mudrā; it destroys the diseases of the Yogins. (9)

अथ उड्डीयानबन्धः ।

उदरे पश्चिमं तानं नाभेरूर्ध्वं तु कारयेत् ।
उड्डीनं कुरुते यस्मादविश्रान्तं महाखगः ।
उड्डीयानं त्वसौ बन्धो मृत्युमातङ्गकेसरी ॥ १० ॥

(3) UḌḌĪYĀNA-BANDHA

Contract the bowels equably above and below the navel towards the back, so that the abdominal viscera may touch the back. He who practises this Uḍḍīyāna (Flying up), without ceasing, conquers death. [The Great Bird (Breath), by this process, is instantly forced up into the Suṣumṇā, and flies (moves) constantly therein only.] (10)

अथ उड्डीयानबन्धस्य फलकथनम् ।

समग्राद् बन्धनाद्ध्येतदुड्डीयानं विशिष्यते ।
उड्डीयने समभ्यस्ते मुक्तिः स्वाभाविकी भवेत् ॥११॥

Its benefits

Of all Bandhas, this is the best. The complete practice of this makes emancipation easy. (11)

अथ जालन्धरबन्धकथनम् ।

कण्ठसंकोचनं कृत्वा चिबुकं हृदये न्यसेत् ।
जालन्धरे कृते बन्धे षोडशाधारबन्धनम् ।
जालन्धरमहामुद्रा मृत्योश्च क्षयकारिणी ॥ १२ ॥

(4) JĀLANDHARA

Contracting the throat, place the chin on the chest. This is called Jālandhara. By this Bandha the sixteen Ādhāras are closed. This Mahā-mudrā destroys death. (12)

अथ जालन्धरबन्धस्य फलकथनम् ।

सिद्धो जालन्धरो बन्धो योगिनां सिद्धिदायकः ।
षण्मासमभ्यसेद्यो हि स सिद्धो नात्र संशयः ॥ १३ ॥

Its benefits

This success-giving Jȃlandhara when practised well for six months, the man becomes an adept without doubt. (13)

अथ मूलबन्धकथनम् ।

पार्ष्णिना वामपादस्य योनिमाकुञ्चयेत्ततः ।
नाभिग्रन्थिं मेरुदण्डे सुधीः संपीड्य यत्नतः ॥ १४ ॥
मेढ्रं दक्षिणगुल्फे तु दृढबन्धं समाचरेत् ।
जराविनाशिनी मुद्रा मूलबन्धो निगद्यते ॥ १५ ॥

(5) MŪLABANDHA

Press with the heel of the left foot the region between the anus and the scrotum, and contract the rectum; carefully press the intestines near the navel on the spine; and put the right heel on the organ of generation or pubes. This is called Mūlabandha, destroyer of decay. (14—15)

अथ मूलबन्धस्य फलकथनम् ।

संसारसागरं तर्तुमभिलष्यति यः पुमान् ।
सुगुप्तो विरले भूत्वा मुद्रामेतां समभ्यसेत् ॥ १६ ॥
अभ्यासाद् बन्धनस्यास्य मरुत्सिद्धिर्भवेद् ध्रुवम् ।
साधयेद् यत्नतस्तर्हि मौनी तु विजितालसः ॥ १७ ॥

Its benefits

The person who desires to cross the ocean of Saṃsāra, let him go to a retired place, and practise in secrecy this mudrā. By the practice of it, the Vāyu (Prāṇa) is controlled undoubtedly; let one silently practise this, without laziness, and with care. (16—17)

अथ महाबन्धकथनम् ।

वामपादस्य गुल्फेन पायुमूलं निरोधयेत् ।
दक्षपादेन तद् गुल्फं सुधीः संपीड्य यत्नतः ॥ १८ ॥
शनकैश्चालयेत्पार्ष्णिं योनिमाकुञ्चयेच्छनैः ।
जालन्धरे धरेत्प्राणं महाबन्धो निगद्यते ॥ १९ ॥

(6) MAHĀBANDHA

Close the anal orifice by the heel of the left foot, press that heel with the right foot carefully, move slowly the muscles of the rectum, and slowly contract the muscles of the yoni or perineum (space between the anus and the Scrotum): restrain the breath by Jālan-dhara. This is called Mahābandha. (18—19)

अथ महाबन्धस्य फलकथनम् ।

महाबन्धः परो बन्धो जरामरणनाशनः ।
प्रसादादस्य बन्धस्य साधयेत्सर्ववाञ्छितम् ॥ २० ॥

Its benefits

The Mahābandha is the Greatest Bandha; it destroys decay and death: by virtue of this Bandha a man accomplishes all his desires. (20)

अथ महावेधकथनम् ।

रूपयौवनलावण्यं नारीणां पुरुषं विना ।
मूलबन्धमहाबन्धौ महावेधं विना तथा ॥ २१ ॥
महाबन्धं समासाद्य चरेदुड्डानकुम्भकम् ।
महावेधः समाख्यातो योगिनां सिद्धिदायकः ॥ २२ ॥

(7) MAHĀVEDHA

As the beauty, youth and charms of women are in vain without men, so are Mūlabandha and Mahābandha without Mahāvedha. Sit first in Mahābandha posture, then restrain breath by Uḍḍāna Kumbhaka. This is called Mahāvedha—the giver of success to the Yogins. (21—22)

अथ महावेधस्य फलकथनम् ।

महाबन्धमूलबन्धौ महावेधसमन्वितौ ।
प्रत्यहं कुरुते यस्तु स योगी योगवित्तमः ॥ २३ ॥
न मृत्युतो भयं तस्य न जरा तस्य विद्यते ।
गोपनीयः प्रयत्नेन वेधोऽयं योगिपुंगवैः ॥ २४ ॥

Its benefits

The Yogin who daily practises Mahābandha and Mūlabandha, accompanied with Mahāvedha, is the best of the Yogins. For him there is no fear of death, and decay does not approach him: this Vedha should be kept carefully secret by the Yogins. (23—24)

अथ खेचरीमुद्राकथनम् ।

जिह्वाधो नाडीं संछिन्नां रसनां चालयेत्सदा ।
दोहयेन्नवनीतेन लौहयन्त्रेण कर्षयेत् ॥ २५ ॥

(8) KHECARĪ MUDRĀ

Cut the lower tendon of the tongue, and move the tongue constantly ; rub it with fresh butter, and draw it out (to lengthen it) with an iron instrument. (25)

N.B.—This is the preliminary to Khecarī Mudrā. Its object is so to lengthen the tongue, that when drawn out it may touch with its tip the space between the eye-brows. This can be done by cutting away the lower tendon. It takes about three years to cut away the whole tendon. I saw my Guru doing it in this wise. On every Monday he used to cut the tendon one-twelfth of an inch deep and sprinkle salt over it, so that the cut portions might not join together. Then rubbing the tongue with butter he used to pull it out. Peculiar iron instruments are employed for this purpose; the painful process is repeated every week till the tongue can be stretched out to the requisite length.

एवं नित्यं समभ्यासाल्लम्बिका दीर्घतां व्रजेत् ।
यावद् गच्छेद् भ्रुवोर्मध्ये तदाऽऽगच्छति खेचरी ॥ २६ ॥

By practising this always, the tongue becomes long, and when it reaches the space between the eyebrows, then the Khecarī is accomplished. (26)

रसनां तालुमध्ये तु शनैः शनैः प्रवेशयेत् ।
कपालकुहरे जिह्वा प्रविष्टा विपरीतगा ।
भ्रुवोर्मध्ये गता दृष्टिर्मुद्रा भवति खेचरी ॥ २७ ॥

Then (the tongue being lengthened) practise, turning it upwards and backwards so as to touch the palate, till at length it reaches the holes of the nostrils opening into the mouth. Close those holes with the tongue (thus stopping inspiration), and fix the gaze on the space between the eyebrows. This is called Khecarī. (27)

अथ खेचरीमुद्रायाः फलकथनम् ।

न च मूर्च्छा क्षुधा तृष्णा नैवालस्यं प्रजायते ।
न च रोगो जरा मृत्युर्देवदेहः स जायते ॥ २८ ॥

Its benefits

By this practice there is neither fainting, nor hunger, nor thirst, nor laziness. There comes neither disease, nor decay, nor death. The body becomes divine. (28)

नाग्निना दह्यते गात्रं न शोषयति मारुतः ।
न देहं क्लेदयन्त्यापो दशेन्न च भुजङ्गमः ॥ २९ ॥

The body cannot be burned by fire, nor dried up by air, nor wetted by water, nor bitten by snakes. (29)

लावण्यं च भवेद् गात्रे समाधिर्जायते ध्रुवम् ।
कपालवक्त्रसंयोगे रसना रसमाप्नुयात् ॥ ३० ॥

The body becomes beautiful; Samâdhi is verily attained, and the tongue touching the holes in the roof (of the mouth) obtains various juices (it drinks nectar). (30)

नानारससमुद्भूतमानन्दं च दिने दिने ।
आदौ तु लवणं क्षारं ततस्तिक्तकषायकम् ॥ ३१ ॥
नवनीतं घृतं क्षीरं दधितक्रमधूनि च ।
द्राक्षारसं च पीयूषं जायते रसनोदकम् ॥ ३२ ॥

Various juices being produced, day by day the man experiences new sensations; first, he experiences a saltish taste, then alkaline, then bitter, then astringent, then he feels the taste of butter, then of ghee, then of milk, then of curds, then of whey, then of honey, then of palm juice, and, lastly, arises the taste of nectar. (31—32)

अथ विपरीतकरणीमुद्राकथनम् ।

नाभिमूले वसेत्सूर्यस्तालुमूले च चन्द्रमाः ।
अमृतं ग्रसते सूर्यस्ततो मृत्युवशो नरः ॥ ३३ ॥
उर्ध्वं च योजयेत्सूर्यं चन्द्रं चाप्यध आनयेत् ।
विपरीतकरी मुद्रा सर्वतन्त्रेषु गोपिता ॥ ३४ ॥
भूमौ शिरश्च संस्थाप्य करयुग्मं समाहितः ।
उर्ध्वपादः स्थिरो भूत्वा विपरीतकरी मता ॥ ३५ ॥

(9) VIPARĪTAKARAṆĪ

The sun (the solar Nādī or plexus) dwells at the root of the navel, and the moon at the root of the palate ; as the sun eats up the nectar man becomes subject to death. The process by which the sun is brought upward and the moon carried downward is called Viparītakaraṇī. It is a sacred Mudrā in all the Tantras. Place the head on the ground, with hands spread, raise the legs up, and thus remain steady. This is called Viparītakaraṇī. (33—35)

अथ विपरीतकरणीमुद्रायाः फलकथनम् ।

मुद्रां च साधयेन्नित्यं जरां मृत्युं च नाशयेत् ।
स सिद्धः सर्वलोकेषु प्रलयेऽपि न सीदति ॥ ३६ ॥

Its benefits

By the constant practice of this Mudrâ, decay and death are destroyed. He becomes an adept, and does not perish even at pralaya. (36)

अथ योनिमुद्राकथनम् ।

सिद्धासनं समासाद्य कर्णचक्षुर्नसामुखम् ।
अङ्गुष्ठतर्जनीमध्यानामाद्यैः पिदधीत वै ॥ ३७ ॥
प्राणमाकृष्य काकीभिरपाने योजयेत्ततः ।
षट् चक्राणि क्रमाद्ध्यात्वा हुं हंसमनुना सुधीः ॥३८॥
चैतन्यमानयेद्देवीं निद्रिता या भुजङ्गिनी ।
जीवेन सहितां शक्तिं समुत्थाप्य कराम्बुजे ॥ ३९ ॥
स्वयं शक्तिमयो भूत्वा परं शिवेन संगमम् ।
नानासुखं विहारं च चिन्तयेत्परमं सुखम् ॥ ४० ॥
शिवशक्तिसमायोगादेकान्तं भुवि भावयेत् ।
आनन्दमानसो भूत्वा चाहं ब्रह्मेति संभवेत् ॥ ४१ ॥
योनिमुद्रा परा गोप्या देवानामपि दुर्लभा ।
सकृत्तु लब्धसंसिद्धिः समाधिस्थः स एव हि ॥ ४२ ॥

(10) YONIMUDRĀ

Sitting in Siddhâsana, close the ears with the thumbs, the eyes with the index fingers, the nostrils with the middle fingers, the upper lip with the ring-fingers, and the lower lip with the little fingers. Draw in the Prāṇa-Vāyu by Kākī-mudrā (as in verse 86) and join it with the Apāna-Vāyu; contemplating the six cakras in their order, let the wise one awaken the sleeping serpent-goddess Kuṇḍalinī, by repeating the mantra Huṃ (हुं), and Haṁsa (हंस:), and raising the S'akti (Force-kuṇḍalinī) with the jīva, place her at the thousand-petalled lotus. Being himself full of S'akti, being joined with the great S'iva, let him think of the Supreme Bliss. Let him contemplate on the union of S'iva (spirit) and S'akti (force or energy) in this world. Being himself all bliss, let him realise that he is the Brahman. This Yonimudrā is a great secret, difficult to be obtained even by the Devas. By once obtaining perfection in its practice, one enters verily into Samādhi. (37—42)

अथ योनिमुद्राफलकथनम् ।

ब्रह्महा भ्रूणहा चैव सुरापो गुरुतल्पगः ।
एतैः पापैर्न लिप्येत योनिमुद्रानिबन्धनात् ॥ ४३ ॥

यानि पापानि घोराणि तूपपापानि यानि च ।
तानि सर्वाणि नश्यन्ति योनिमुद्रानिबन्धनात् ।
तस्मादभ्यसनं कुर्याद्यदि मुक्तिं समिच्छति ॥ ४४ ॥

Its benefits

By the practice of this Mudrā, one is never polluted by the sins of killing a Brāhmaṇa, killing a fœtus, drinking liquor, or polluting the bed of the Preceptor. All the mortal sins and the venal sins are completely destroyed by the practice of this Mudrā. Let him therefore practise it, if he wishes for emancipation. (43—44)

अथ वज्रोलीमुद्राकथनम् ।

आश्रित्य भूमिं करयोस्तलाभ्यामूर्ध्वं क्षिपेत्पादयुगं शिरः खे ।
शक्तिप्रबुद्धयै चिरजीवनाय वज्रोलिमुद्रां मुनयो वदन्ति ॥४५॥

(11) VAJROLĪ MUDRĀ

Place the two palms on the ground, raise the legs in the air upward, the head not touching the earth. This awakens the S'akti, causes long life, and is called Vajrolī by the sages. (45)

अथ वज्रोलीमुद्रायाः फलकथनम् ।

योगश्रेष्ठो ह्ययं योगो योगिनां मुक्तिकारणम् ।
अयं हितप्रदो योगो योगिनां सिद्धिदायकः ॥ ४६ ॥
एतद्योगप्रसादेन बिन्दुसिद्धिर्भवेद् ध्रुवम् ।
सिद्धे बिन्दौ महायत्ने किं न सिध्यति भूतले ॥ ४७ ॥
भोगेन महता युक्तो यदि मुद्रां समाचरेत् ।
तथाऽपि सकला सिद्धिर्जायते तस्य निश्चितम् ॥ ४८॥

Its benefits

This practice is the highest of Yogas; it causes emancipation, and this beneficial Yoga gives perfection to the Yogins. By virtue of this Yoga, the Bindu-siddhi (retention of seed) is obtained, and when that siddhi is obtained what else can he not attain in this world. Though immersed in manifold pleasures, if he practises this Mudrā, he attains verily all perfections. (46—48)

अथ शक्तिचालनीमुद्राकथनम् ।

मूलाधार आत्मशक्तिः कुण्डली परदेवता ।
शयिता भुजगाकारा सार्धत्रिवलयान्विता ॥ ४९ ॥

(12) S'AKTICĀLANĪ

The great goddess Kuṇḍalinī, the energy of Self, ātma-s'akti (spiritual force), sleeps in the Mūlādhāra (rectum); she has the form of a serpent having three coils and a half. (49)

यावत्सा निद्रिता देहे तावज्जीवः पशुर्यथा ।
ज्ञानं न जायते तावत्कोटियोगं समभ्यसेत् ॥ ५० ॥

So long as she is asleep in the body, the Jīva is a mere animal, and true knowledge does not arise, though he may practise ten millions of Yoga. (50)

उद्घाटयेत्कवाटं च तथा कुञ्चिकया हठात् ।
कुण्डलिन्याः प्रबोधेन ब्रह्मद्वारं प्रभेदयेत् ॥ ५१ ॥

As by a key a door is opened, so by awakening the Kuṇḍalinī by Haṭha Yoga, the door of Brahman is unlocked. (51)

नाभिं संवेष्ट्य वस्त्रेण न च नग्नो बहिःस्थितः ।
गोपनीयगृहे स्थित्वा शक्तिचालनमभ्यसेत् ॥ ५२ ॥

Encircling the loins with a piece of cloth, seated in a secret room, not naked in an outer room, let him practise the S'akticālana. (52)

वितस्तिप्रमितं दीर्घं विस्तारे चतुरङ्गुलम् ।
मृदुलं धवलं सूक्ष्मं वेष्टनाम्बरलक्षणम् ।
एवमम्बरयुक्तं च कटिसूत्रेण योजयेत् ॥ ५३ ॥

One cubit long, and four fingers (3 inches) wide, should be the encircling cloth, soft, white and of fine texture. Join this cloth with the Kaṭi-Sūtra (a string worn round the loins). (53)

संलिप्य भस्मना गात्रं सिद्धासनमथाचरेत् ।
नासाभ्यां प्राणमाकृष्याप्यपाने योजयेद् बलात् ॥५४॥
तावदाकुञ्चयेद् गुह्यमश्विनीमुद्रया शनैः ।
यावद्गच्छेत्सुषुम्णायां हठाद्वायुः प्रकाशयेत् ॥ ५५ ॥

Smear the body with ashes, sit in Siddhāsana-posture, drawing the Prāṇa-Vāyu with the nostrils, forcibly join it with the Apāna. Contract the rectum slowly by the As'vinī Mudrā, till the Vāyu enters the Suṣumṇā, and manifests its presence. (54—55)

तदा वायुप्रबन्धेन कुम्भिका च भुजङ्गिनी ।
बद्धश्वासस्ततो भूत्वा चोर्ध्वमार्गं प्रपद्यते ॥ ५६ ॥

By restraining the breath by Kumbhaka in this way, the serpent Kuṇḍalinī, feeling suffocated, awakes and rises upwards to the Brahmarandhra. (56)

विना शक्तिचालनेन योनिमुद्रा न सिध्यति ।
आदौ चालनमभ्यस्य योनिमुद्रां समभ्यसेत् ॥ ५७ ॥

Without the S'akticālana, the Yoni-Mudrā is not complete or perfected; first the Cālana should be practised, and then the Yoni-Mudrā. (57)

इति ते कथितं चण्डकपाले शक्तिचालनम् ।
गोपनीयं प्रयत्नेन दिने दिने समभ्यसेत् ॥ ५८ ॥

O Caṇḍa-Kapāli! thus have I taught thee the S'akticālana. Preserve it with care and practise it daily. (58)

अथ शक्तिचालनीमुद्रायाः फलकथनम् ।

मुद्रेयं परमा गोप्या जरामरणनाशिनी ।
तस्मादभ्यसनं कार्यं योगिभिः सिद्धिकाङ्क्षिभिः ॥५९॥

Its benefits

This mudrā should be kept carefully concealed. It destroys decay and death.

Therefore the Yogin, desirous of perfection, should practise it. (59)

नित्यं योऽभ्यसते योगी सिद्धिस्तस्य करे स्थिता ।
तस्य विग्रहसिद्धिः स्याद्रोगाणां संक्षयो भवेत् ॥ ६० ॥

The Yogin who practises this daily, acquires adeptship, attains Vigraha-siddhi and all his diseases are cured. (60)

अथ ताडागीमुद्राकथनम् ।

उदरं पश्चिमोत्तानं तडागाकृति कारयेत् ।
ताडागी सा परा मुद्रा जरामृत्युविनाशिनी ॥ ६१ ॥

(13) TĀDĀGĪ-MUDRĀ

Make the abdomen look quite hollow just like a tank. This is Tādāgī (Tank) Mudrā, destroyer of decay and death. (61)

अथ माण्डुकीमुद्राकथनम् ।

मुखं संमुद्रितं कृत्वा जिह्वामूलं प्रचालयेत् ।
शनैर्ग्रसेत्तदमृतं माण्डुकीं मुद्रिकां विदुः ॥ ६२ ॥

(14) MĀṆḌUKĪ-MUDRĀ

Closing the mouth, move the tongue towards the palate, and taste slowly the nectar (flowing from the Thousand-petalled Lotus). This is Frog-mudrā. (62)

अथ माण्डुकीमुद्रायाः फलकथनम् ।

वलितं पलितं नैव जायते नित्ययौवनम् ।
न केशे जायते पाको यः कुर्यान्नित्यमाण्डुकीम् ॥६३॥

Its benefits

The body never sickens nor becomes old, and it retains perpetual youth; the hair of him who practises this never grows grey. (63)

अथ शांभवीमुद्राकथनम् ।

नेत्रान्तरं समालोक्य चात्मारामं निरीक्षयेत् ।
सा भवेच्छांभवी मुद्रा सर्वतन्त्रेषु गोपिता ॥ ६४ ॥

(15) S'ĀṂBHAVĪ-MUDRĀ

Fixing the gaze between the eye-brows, behold the Self-existent. This is S'āṃbhavī, secret in all the Tantras. (64)

अथ शांभवीमुद्रायाः फलकथनम् ।

वेदशास्त्रपुराणानि सामान्यगणिका इव ।
इयं तु शांभवी मुद्रा गुप्ता कुलवधूरिव ॥ ६५ ॥

Its benefits

The Vedas, the scriptures, the Purāṇas are like public women, but this S'āṃbhavī should be guarded as if it were a lady of a respectable family. (65)

स एव ह्यादिनाथश्च स च नारायणः स्वयम् ।
स च ब्रह्मा सृष्टिकारी यो मुद्रां वेत्ति शांभवीम् ॥ ६६ ॥

He, who knows this S'āṃbhavī, is like the Ādinātha, he is Nārāyaṇa, he is Brahmā, the Creator. (66)

सत्यं सत्यं पुनः सत्यं सत्यमाह महेश्वरः ।
शांभवीं यो विजानीयात्स च ब्रह्म न चान्यथा ॥ ६७ ॥

Mahes'vara has said, "Truly, truly, and again truly, he who knows the S'āṃbhavī, is Brahman. There is no doubt of this." (67)

अथ पञ्चधारणामुद्राकथनम् ।

कथिता शांभवी मुद्रा शृणुष्व पञ्चधारणाम् ।
धारणानि समासाद्य किं न सिध्यति भूतले ॥ ६८ ॥

(16) THE FIVE DHĀRAṆĀ-MUDRĀS

The S'āṃbhavī has been explained; hear now the five Dhāraṇās. Learning these five

Dhāraṇās, what cannot be accomplished in this world? (68)

अनेन नरदेहेन स्वर्गेषु गमनागमम् ।
मनोगतिर्भवेत्तस्य खेचरत्वं न चान्यथा ॥ ६९ ॥

By this human body one can visit and re-visit Svargaloka, he can go wherever he likes, as swiftly as mind, he acquires the faculty of moving in the air. [These five Dhāraṇās are: Pārthivī (Earthy), Āmbhasī (Watery), Vāyavī (Aerial), Āgneyī (Fiery), and Ākāśī (Ethereal).] (69)

अथ पार्थिवीधारणामुद्राकथनम् ।

यत्तत्त्वं हरितालदेशरचितं भौमं लकारान्वितं
वेदास्रं कमलासनेन सहितं कृत्वा हृदि स्थापितम् ।
प्राणं तत्र विलीय पञ्च घटिकाश्चित्तान्वितं धारये-
देषा स्तम्भकरी सदा क्षितिजयं कुर्यादधोधारणा ॥७०॥

(*a*) PĀRTHIVĪ

The Pṛithivī-Tattva has the colour of orpiment (yellow), the letter (la) ल is its secret symbol or seed (बीज), its form is four-sided, and Brahmā, its presiding deity. Place this Tattva in the heart, and fix by Kumbhaka the Prāṇa-Vāyus and the Citta there for the period of five ghaṭikās (2½ hours). This is called Adho-dhāraṇā. By this, one conquers the Earth, and no earthy-elements can injure him ; and it causes steadiness. (70)

अथ पार्थिवीधारणामुद्रायाः फलकथनम् ।

पार्थिवीधारणामुद्रां यः करोति च नित्यशः ।
मृत्युंजयः स्वयं सोऽपि स सिद्धो विचरेद् भुवि ॥७१॥

Its benefits

He who practises daily this dhāraṇā, becomes like the conqueror of Death ; as an Adept he walks this earth. (71)

अथ आम्भसीधारणामुद्राकथनम् ।

शङ्खेन्दुप्रतिमं च कुन्दधवलं तत्त्वं किलालं शुभं
तत्पीयूषवकारबीजसहितं युक्तं सदा विष्णुना ।
प्राणं तत्र विलीय पञ्च घटिकाश्चित्तान्वितं धारये-
देषा दुःसहतापपापहरणी स्यादाम्भसी धारणा ॥७२ ॥

(*b*) ĀMBHASĪ

The Water-Tattva is white like the Kunda-flower or a conch or the moon, its form is circular like the moon, the letter व (va) is the seed of this ambrosial element, and Viṣṇu is its presiding deity. By Yoga, produce the water-tattva in the heart, and fix there the Prāṇa with the Citta (consciousness), for five ghaṭikās, practising Kumbhaka. This is Watery Dhāraṇā; it is the destroyer of all sorrows. Water cannot injure him who practises this. (72)

अथ आम्भसीमुद्रायाः फलकथनम् ।

आम्भसीं परमां मुद्रां यो जानाति स योगवित् ।
गभीरे च जले घोरे मरणं तस्य नो भवेत् ॥ ७३ ॥
इयं तु परमा मुद्रा गोपनीया प्रयत्नतः ।
प्रकाशात्सिद्धिहानिः स्यात्सत्यं वच्मि च तत्त्वतः ॥७४॥

Its benefits

The Āmbhasī is a great mudrā; the Yogin who knows it, never meets death even in the deepest water. This should be kept carefully concealed. By revealing it success is lost, verily I tell you the truth. (73—74)

अथ आग्नेयीधारणामुद्राकथनम् ।

यन्नाभिस्थितमिन्द्रगोपसदृशं बीजं त्रिकोणान्वितं
तत्त्वं वह्निमयं प्रदीप्तमरुणं रुद्रेण यत्सिद्धिदम् ।
प्राणं तत्र विलीय पञ्च घटिकाश्चित्तान्वितं धारये-
देषा कालगभीरभीतिहरणी वैश्वानरी धारणा ॥ ७५ ॥

(c) ĀGNEYĪ

The Fire-tattva is situated at the navel, its colour is red like the Indra-gopa insect, its form is triangular, its seed is र (ra), its presiding deity is Rudra. It is refulgent like the sun, and the giver of success. Fix the Prāṇa along with the Citta on this Tattva for five ghaṭikās. This is called Fire-dhāraṇā, destroyer of the fear of dreadful death, and fire cannot injure him. (75)

अथ आग्नेयीधारणामुद्रायाः फलकथनम् ।

प्रदीप्ते ज्वलिते वह्नावपि चेत्साधकः पतेत् ।
एतन्मुद्राप्रसादेन स जीवति न मृत्युभाक् ॥ ७६ ॥

Its benefits

Even if the practitioner is thrown into burning fire, by virtue of this Mudrā he remains alive, without fear of death. (76)

अथ वायवीधारणामुद्राकथनम् ।

यद्भिन्नाञ्जनपुञ्जसंनिभमिदं धूम्रावभासं परं
तत्त्वं सत्त्वमयं यकारसहितं यत्रेश्वरो देवता ।
प्राणं तत्र विलीय पञ्च घटिकाश्चित्तान्वितं धारये-
देषा खे गमनं करोति यमिनां स्याद्वायवी धारणा ॥ ७७ ॥

(*d*) VĀYAVĪ

The Air-tattva is black as unguent for the eyes (collirium), the letter य (ya) is its seed, and Īs'vara its presiding deity. This Tattva is full of Sattva quality. Fix the Prāṇa and the Citta for five ghaṭikās on this Tattva. This is Vāyavī-dhāraṇā. By this, the practitioner walks in the air. (77)

अथ वायवीधारणामुद्रायाः फलकथनम् ।

इयं तु परमा मुद्रा जरामृत्युविनाशिनी ।
वायुना म्रियते नापि खे गतेश्च प्रदायिनी ॥ ७८ ॥
शठाय भक्तिहीनाय न देया यस्य कस्यचित् ।
दत्ते च सिद्धिहानिः स्यात्सत्यं वच्मि च चण्ड ते ॥७९॥

Its benefits

This great Mudrā destroys decay and death. Its practitioner is never killed by any aerial disturbances; by its virtue one walks in the air. This should not be taught to the wicked or to those devoid of faith. By so doing success is lost; Oh Caṇḍa! this is verily the truth. (78—79)

अथ आकाशीधारणामुद्राकथनम् ।

यत्सिन्धौ वरशुद्धवारिसदृशं व्योमाख्यमुद्भासते
तत्त्वं देवसदाशिवेन सहितं बीजं हकारान्वितम् ।
प्राणं तत्र विलीय पञ्च घटिकाश्चित्तान्वितं धारये-
देषा मोक्षकवाटभेदनकरी कुर्यान्नभोधारणाम् ॥ ८० ॥

(e) ĀKĀS'Ī DHĀRAṆĀ

The Ākās'a-tattva has the colour of pure sea-water, ह (ha) is its seed, its presiding deity is Sadās'iva. Fix the Prāṇa along with Citta for five ghaṭikās in this tattva. This is Ether-dhāraṇā. It opens the gates of emancipation. (80)

अथ आकाशीधारणामुद्रायाः फलकथनम् ।

आकाशीधारणां मुद्रां यो वेत्ति स च योगवित् ।
न मृत्युजरिते तस्य प्रलये नावसीदति ॥ ८१ ॥

Its benefits

He who knows this Dhāraṇā is the real Yogin. Death and old age do not approach him, nor does he perish at the Pralaya. (81)

अथ अश्विनीमुद्राकथनम् ।

आकुञ्चयेद् गुदद्वारं प्रकाशयेत्पुनः पुनः ।
सा भवेदश्विनीमुद्रा शक्तिप्रबोधकारिणी ॥ ८२ ॥

(21) AS'VINĪ-MUDRĀ

Contract and dilate the anal aperture again and again, this is called As'vinī-mudrā. It awakens the S'akti (Kuṇḍalinī). (82)

अश्विनीमुद्रायाः फलकथनम् ।

अश्विनी परमा मुद्रा गुह्यरोगविनाशिनी ।
बलपुष्टिकरी चैवाप्यकालमरणं हरेत् ॥ ८३ ॥

Its benefits

This As'vinī is a great mudrā ; it destroys all diseases of the rectum ; it gives strength and vigour, and prevents premature death. (83)

अथ पाशिनीमुद्राकथनम् ।

कण्ठपृष्ठे क्षिपेत्पादौ पाशवद् दृढबन्धनम् ।
सैव स्यात्पाशिनीमुद्रा शक्तिप्रबोधकारिणी ॥ ८४ ॥

(22) PĀS'ĪNĪ-MUDRĀ

Throw the two legs on the neck towards the back, holding them strongly together like a Pāsa (a noose). This is called Pās'inī-mudrā; it awakens the S'akti (Kuṇḍalinī). (84)

अथ पाशिनीमुद्रायाः फलकथनम् ।

पाशिनी महती मुद्रा बलपुष्टिविधायिनी ।
साधनीया प्रयत्नेन साधकैः सिद्धिकाङ्क्षिभिः ॥ ८५ ॥

Its benefits

This grand Mudrā gives strength and nourishment. It should be practised with care by those who desire success. (85)

अथ काकीमुद्राकथनम् ।

काकचञ्चुवदास्येन पिबेद्वायुं शनैः शनैः ।
काकीमुद्रा भवेदेषा सर्वरोगविनाशिनी ॥ ८६ ॥

(23) KĀKĪ-MUDRĀ

Contract the lips, like the beak of a crow, and drink (draw in) the air slowly and slowly. This is Kākī (crow) mudrā, destroyer of all diseases. (86)

अथ काकीमुद्रायाः फलकथनम् ।

काकीमुद्रा परा मुद्रा सर्वतन्त्रेषु गोपिता ।
अस्याः प्रसादमात्रेण न रोगी काकवद् भवेत् ॥ ८७ ॥

Its benefits

The Kākī-mudrā is a great Mudrā, kept secret in all Tantras. By virtue of this, one becomes free from disease like a crow. (87)

अथ मातङ्गिनीमुद्राकथनम् ।

कण्ठदघ्ने जले स्थित्वा नासाभ्यां जलमाहरेत् ।
मुखान्निर्गमयेत्पश्चात्पुनर्वक्त्रेण चाहरेत् ॥ ८८ ॥
नासाभ्यां रेचयेत्पश्चात्कुर्यादेवं पुनः पुनः ।
मातङ्गिनी परा मुद्रा जरामृत्युविनाशिनी ॥ ८९ ॥

(24) MĀTAṄGINĪ-MUDRĀ

Stand in neck-deep water, draw in the water through the nostrils, and throw it out by the mouth. Then draw in the water through [the mouth and expel it through] the nostrils. Let one repeat this again and again. This is called Elephant-mudrā, destroyer of decay and death. (88—89)

अथ मातङ्गिनीमुद्रायाः फलकथनम् ।

विरले निर्जने देशे स्थित्वा चैकाग्रमानसः ।
कुर्यान्मातङ्गिनीं मुद्रां मातङ्ग इव जायते ॥ ९० ॥
यत्र यत्र स्थितो योगी सुखमत्यन्तमश्नुते ।
तस्मात्सर्वप्रयत्नेन साधयेन्मुद्रिकां पराम् ॥ ९१ ॥

Its benefits

In a solitary place, free from human intrusion, one should practise with fixed attention this Elephant-mudrā; by so doing, he becomes strong like the elephant. Wherever he may be, by this process the Yogin enjoys great pleasure; therefore this mudrā should be practised with great care. (90—91)

अथ भुजङ्गिनीमुद्राकथनम् ।

वक्त्रं किंचित्सुप्रसार्य चानिलं गलया पिबेत् ।
सा भवेद् भुजगी मुद्रा जरामृत्युविनाशिनी ॥ ९२ ॥

(25) BHUJAṄGINĪ-MUDRĀ

Extending the face a little forward, let him drink (draw in) air through the gullet; this is called Serpent-mudrā, destroyer of decay and death. (92)

अथ भुजङ्गिनीमुद्रायाः फलकथनम् ।

यावन्तश्चोदरे रोगा अजीर्णाद्या विशेषतः ।
तान्सर्वान्नाशयेदाशु यत्र मुद्रा भुजङ्गिनी ॥ ९३ ॥

Its benefits

This Serpent-mudrā quickly destroys all stomach diseases, especially indigestion, dyspepsia, etc. (93)

अथ मुद्राणां फलकथनम् ।

इदं तु मुद्रापटलं कथितं चण्ड ते शुभम् ।
वल्लभं सर्वसिद्धानां जरामरणनाशनम् ॥ ९४ ॥

THE BENEFITS OF MUDRĀS

O Caṇḍa-Kāpāli ! thus have I recited to thee the chapter on Mudrās. This is beloved of all adepts, and destroys decay and death. (94)

शठाय भक्तिहीनाय न देयं यस्य कस्यचित् ।
गोपनीयं प्रयत्नेन दुर्लभं मरुतामपि ॥ ९५ ॥

This should not be taught indiscriminately, nor to a wicked person, nor to one devoid of faith; this secret should be preserved with great care; it is difficult to be attained even by the Devas. (95)

ऋजवे शान्तचित्ताय गुरुभक्तिपराय च ।
कुलीनाय प्रदातव्यं भोगमुक्तिप्रदायकम् ॥ ९६ ॥

These Mudrâs which give happiness and emancipation should be taught to a guileless, calm and peace-minded person, who is devoted to his Teacher and comes of good family. (96)

मुद्राणां पटलं ह्येतत्सर्वव्याधिविनाशनम् ।
नित्यमभ्यासशीलस्य जाठराग्निविवर्धनम् ॥ ९७ ॥

These Mudrâs destroy all diseases. They increase the gastric fire of him who practises them daily. (97)

न तस्य जायते मृत्युस्तथाऽस्य न जरादिकम् ।
नाग्निवारिभयं तस्य वायोरपि कुतो भयम् ॥ ९८ ॥

To him death never comes, nor decay, etc.; there is no fear to him from fire and water, nor from air. (98)

कासः श्वासः प्लीहा कुष्ठं श्लेष्मरोगाश्च विंशतिः ।
मुद्राणां साधनाच्चैव विनश्यन्ति न संशयः ॥ ९९ ॥

Cough, asthma, enlargement of the spleen, leprosy, phlegm-diseases of twenty sorts, are verily destroyed by the practice of these Mudrās. (99)

बहुना किमिहोक्तेन सारं वच्मि च चण्ड ते ।
नास्ति मुद्रासमं किंचित्सिद्धिदं क्षितिमण्डले ॥१००॥

इति श्रीघेरण्डसंहितायां घेरण्डचण्डसंवादे घटस्थ-
योगप्रकरणे मुद्राप्रयोगो नाम तृतीयोपदेशः ।

O Caṇḍa! What more shall I tell thee? In short, there is nothing in this world like the Mudrās for giving quick success. (100)

End of the third lesson

चतुर्थोपदेशः ।

LESSON THE FOURTH

PRATYĀHĀRA, OR RESTRAINING THE MIND

घेरण्ड उवाच—

अथातः संप्रवक्ष्यामि प्रत्याहारकमुत्तमम् ।
यस्य विज्ञानमात्रेण कामादिरिपुनाशनम् ॥ १ ॥

GHERAṆḌA SAID

Now I shall tell thee, Pratyāhāra-Yoga the best. By its knowledge, all the passions like lust, etc., are destroyed. (1)

यतो यतो निश्चरति मनश्चञ्चलमस्थिरम् ।
ततस्ततो नियम्यैतदात्मन्येव वशं नयेत् ॥ २ ॥

Let one bring the Citta (thinking principle) under his control by withdrawing it, whenever it wanders away drawn by the various objects of sight. (2)

पुरस्कारं तिरस्कारं सुश्राव्यं वा भयानकम् ।
मनस्तस्मान्नियम्यैतदात्मन्येव वशं नयेत् ॥ ३ ॥

Praise or censure; good speech or bad speech; let one withdraw his mind from all these and bring it under the control of the Self. (3)

सुगन्धे वाऽपि दुर्गन्धे मनो घ्राणेषु जायते ।
तस्मात्प्रत्याहरेदेतदात्मन्येव वशं नयेत् ॥ ४ ॥

From sweet smells or bad smells, by whatever odour the mind may be distracted or attracted, let one withdraw it from that, and bring it under the control of his Self. (4)

मधुराम्लकतिक्तादिरसं गतं यदा मनः ।
तस्मात्प्रत्याहरेदेतदात्मन्येव वशं नयेत् ॥ ५ ॥

इति श्रीघेरण्डसंहितायां घेरण्डचण्डसंवादे घटस्थ-
योगे प्रत्याहारप्रयोगो नाम चतुर्थोपदेशः ।

From sweet or acid tastes, from bitter or astringent tastes, by whatever taste the mind may be attracted, let one withdraw it from that, and bring it within the control of his Self. (5)

End of the fourth lesson

पञ्चमोपदेशः ।

LESSON THE FIFTH

PRĀṆĀYĀMA, OR RESTRAINT OF BREATH

घेरण्ड उवाच—

अथातः संप्रवक्ष्यामि प्राणायामस्य सद्विधिम् ।
यस्य साधनमात्रेण देवतुल्यो भवेन्नरः ॥ १ ॥

GHERAṆḌA SAID

Now I shall tell thee the rules of Prāṇāyāma or regulation of breath. By its practice a man becomes godlike. (1)

आदौ स्थानं तथा कालं मिताहारं तथापरम् ।
नाडीशुद्धिं ततः पश्चात्प्राणायामं च साधयेत् ॥ २ ॥

(Four things are necessary in practising Prāṇāyāma.) First, a good place; second, a suitable time; third, moderate food; and, lastly, the purification of the nāḍīs (Nerve-vessels of the body). (2)

अथ स्थाननिर्णयः ।

दूरदेशे तथाऽरण्ये राजधान्यां जनान्तिके ।
योगारम्भं न कुर्वीत कृतश्चेत्सिद्धिहा भवेत् ॥ ३ ॥

1. PLACE

The practice of Yoga should not be attempted in a far-off country (from home), nor in a forest, nor in a capital city, nor in the midst of a crowd. If one does so, he does not achieve success. (3)

अविश्वासं दूरदेशे अरण्ये रक्षिवर्जितम् ।
लोकारण्ये प्रकाशश्च तस्मात्त्रीणि विवर्जयेत् ॥ ४ ॥

In a distant country, one loses faith (because of the Yoga not being known there); in a forest, one is without protection; and in the midst of a thick population, there is danger of exposure (for then the curious will trouble him). Therefore, let one avoid these three. (4)

सुदेशे धार्मिके राज्ये सुभिक्षे निरुपद्रवे ।
कृत्वा तत्रैकं कुटीरं प्राचीरैः परिवेष्टितम् ॥ ५ ॥

In a good country whose king is just, where food is easily and abundantly procurable, where there are no disturbances, let one erect there a small hut, around it let him raise walls. (5)

वापीकूपतडागं च प्राचीरमध्यवर्ति च ।
नात्युच्चं नातिनिम्नं च कुटीरं कीटवर्जितम् ॥ ६ ॥

And in the centre of the enclosure, let him sink a well and dig a tank. Let the hut be neither very high nor very low; let it be free from insects. (6)

सम्यग्गोमयलिप्तं च कुटीरं तत्र निर्मितम् ।
एवं स्थानेषु गुप्तेषु प्राणायामं समभ्यसेत् ॥ ७ ॥

It should be completely smeared over with cow-dung. In a hut thus built and situated in such a hidden place, let him practise Prāṇāyāma. (7)

अथ कालनिर्णयः ।

हेमन्ते शिशिरे ग्रीष्मे वर्षायां च ऋतौ तथा ।
योगारम्भं न कुर्वीत कृते योगो हि रोगदः ॥ ८ ॥

2. Time

The practice of Yoga should not be commenced in these four seasons out of six: hemanta (winter), s'is'ira (cold), grīṣma (hot), varṣā (rainy). If one begins in these seasons, one will contract diseases. (8)

वसन्ते शरदि प्रोक्तं योगारम्भं समाचरेत् ।
तथा योगी भवेत्सिद्धो रोगान्मुक्तो भवेद् ध्रुवम् ॥ ९ ॥

The practice of Yoga should be commenced by a beginner in the spring (vasanta); and autumn (s'arad). By so doing, he attains success; and verily he does not become liable to diseases. (9)

चैत्रादिफाल्गुनान्ते च माघादिफाल्गुनान्तिके ।
द्वौ द्वौ मासावृतुभागावनुभावश्चतुश्चतुः ॥ १० ॥

The six seasons occur in their order in the twelve months beginning with Caitra and ending with Phālguna: two months being occupied by each season. But each season is experienced for four months, beginning with Māgha and ending with Phālguna. (10)

वसन्तश्चैत्रवैशाखौ ज्येष्ठाषाढा च ग्रीष्मकौ ।
वर्षा श्रावणभाद्राभ्यां शरदाश्विनकार्त्तिकौ ।
मार्गपौषौ च हेमन्तः शिशिरो माघफाल्गुनौ ॥ ११ ॥

SIX SEASONS

The six seasons are as follows:

SEASONS	MONTHS (SANSKRIT)	ENGLISH
Vasanta or Spring	Caitra and Vais'ākha	Mar., Apr.
Grīṣma or Summer	Jyeṣṭha and Āṣāḍha	May, June
Varṣā or Rainy	S'rāvaṇa and Bhādra	July, Aug.
S'arad or Autumn	Ās'vina and Kārttika	Sep., Oct.
Hemanta or Winter	Āgrahāyaṇa and Pauṣa	Nov., Dec.
S'is'ira or Cold	Māgha and Phālguna	Jan., Feb.

(11)

अनुभावं प्रवक्ष्यामि ऋतूनां च यथोदितम् ।
माघादिमाधवान्तेषु वसन्तानुभवं विदुः ॥ १२ ॥
चैत्रादि चाषाढान्तं च निदाघानुभवं विदुः ।
आषाढादि चाश्विनान्तं प्रावृषानुभवं विदुः ॥ १३ ॥
भाद्रादि मार्गशीर्षान्तं शरदोऽनुभवं विदुः ।
कार्त्तिकान्माघमासान्तं हेमन्तानुभवं विदुः ।
मार्गादींश्चतुरो मासाञ्शिशिरानुभवं विदुः ॥ १४ ॥

The Experiencing of Seasons

Now I shall tell thee the experiencing of seasons. They are as follows:

Beginning from Ending with	Season	English
Māgha to Vais'ākha	Vasantānubhava	Jan. to Apr.
Caitra to Āṣāḍha	Grīṣmānubhava	Mar. to June
Āṣāḍha to Ās'vina	Varṣānubhava	June to Sep.
Bhādra to Āgrahāyaṇa	S'aradanubhava	Aug. to Nov.
Kārttika to Māgha	Hemantānubhava	Oct. to Jan.
Āgrahāyaṇa to Phālguṇa	S'is'irānubhava	Nov. to Feb.

(12—14)

वसन्ते वाऽपि शरदि योगारम्भं समाचरेत् ।
तदा योगो भवेत्सिद्धो विनाऽऽयासेन कथ्यते ॥ १५ ॥

The practice of Yoga should be commenced either in Vasanta (spring) or S'arad (autumn). For in these seasons success is attained without much trouble. (15)

अथ मिताहारः ।

मिताहारं विना यस्तु योगारम्भं तु कारयेत् ।
नानारोगो भवेत्तस्य किंचिद्योगो न सिध्यति ॥ १६ ॥

3. Moderation of Diet

He who practises Yoga without moderation of diet, incurs various diseases, and obtains no success. (16)

शाल्यन्नं यवपिंष्टं वा तथा गोधूमपिष्टकम् ।
मुद्गं माषचणकादि शुभ्रं च तुषवर्जितम् ॥ १७ ॥

A Yogin should eat rice, barley (bread), or wheaten bread. He may eat Mudga beans (मुंग, Phaseolus mungo), Māṣa beans (Phaseolus radiatus), gram, etc. These should be clean, white and free from chaff. (17)

पटोलं पनसं मानं कक्कोलं च शुकाशकम् ।
द्राढिकां कर्कटीं रम्भां डुम्बरीं कण्टकण्टकम् ॥ १८ ॥
आमरम्भां भालरम्भां रम्भादण्डं च मूलकम् ।
वार्ताकीं मूलकं चर्द्धिं योगी भक्षणमाचरेत् ॥ १९ ॥

A Yogin may eat paṭola (a kind of cucumber, परवर), jack-fruit, mānakacu (Arum Colocasia), kakkola (a kind of berry), the jujube, the bonduc nut (Bonducella guilandina), cucumber, plantain, fig; the unripe plantain, the small plantain, the plantain stem, and roots, brinjal, and medicinal roots and fruits (*e.g.*, ṛddhi, etc.) (18—19)

बालशाकं कालशाकं तथा पटोलपत्रकम् ।
पञ्चशाकं प्रशंसीयाद्वास्तूकं हिमलोचिकाम् ॥ २० ॥

He may eat green, fresh vegetables बालशाक, black vegetables, the leaves of paṭola, the Vāstūka, and hima-locikā. These are the five s'ākas (vegetable leaves) praised as fit food for Yogins. (20)

शुद्धं सुमधुरं स्निग्धमुदरार्धविवर्जितम् ।
भुज्यते सुरसं प्रीत्या मिताहारमिमं विदुः ॥ २१ ॥

Pure, sweet and cooling food should be eaten to fill half the stomach; eating thus sweet juices with pleasure, and leaving the other half of the stomach empty is called moderation in diet. (21)

अन्नेन पूरयेदर्धं तोयेन तु तृतीयकम् ।
उदरस्य तुरीयांशं संरक्षेद्वायुचारणे ॥ २२ ॥

Half the stomach should be filled with food, one quarter with water; and one quarter should be kept empty for practising prāṇāyāma. (22)

कट्वम्लं लवणं तिक्तं भृष्टं च दधि तक्रकम् ।
शाकोत्कटं तथा मद्यं तालं च पनसं तथा ॥ २३ ॥

Prohibited Foods

In the beginning of Yoga-practice one should discard bitter, acid, salt, pungent and roasted things, curd, whey, heavy vegetables, wine, palmnuts, and over-ripe jack-fruit. (23)

कुलत्थं मसूरं पाण्डुं कूष्माण्डं शाकदण्डकम् ।
तुम्बीकोलकपित्थं च कण्टबिल्वं पलाशकम् ॥ २४ ॥

So also kulattha and masūr beans, pāṇḍu fruit, pumpkins and vegetable stems, gourds, berries, katha-bel, (feronia elephantum), kaṇṭa-bilva and palās'a (Butea frondosa). (24)

कदम्बं जम्बीरं बिम्बं लकुचं लशुनं विषम् ।
कामरङ्गं पियालं च हिङ्गुशाल्मलिकेमुकम् ॥ २५ ॥

So also kadamba (Nauclea cadamba), jambīra (citron), bimba, lakuca (a kind of bread fruit tree), onions, lotus, Kāmaraṅga, piyāla (Buchanania latifolia), hiṅgu (assafoetida), s'ālmalī, kemuka. (25)

योगारम्भे वर्जयेच्च पथिस्त्रीवह्निसेवनम् ।
नवनीतं घृतं क्षीरं शर्कराद्यैक्षवं गुडम् ॥ २६ ॥
पक्वरम्भां नारिकेलं दाडिम्बमशिवासवम् ।
द्राक्षाङ्गुलवनीं धात्रीं रसमम्लविवर्जितम् ॥ २७ ॥

A beginner should avoid much travelling, company of women, and warming himself by fire. So also he should avoid fresh butter, ghee, thickened milk, sugar, and date-sugar, etc., as well as ripe plantain, cocoa-nut, pomegranate, dates, lavanī fruit, āmlaki (myrobalans), and everything containing acid juices. (26—27)

एलाजातिलवङ्गं च पौरुषं जम्बु जाम्बलम् ।
हरीतकीं च खर्जूरं योगी भक्षणमाचरेत् ॥ २८ ॥

But cardamom, jaiphal, cloves, aphrodisiacs or stimulants, the rose-apple, harītakī, and palm dates, a Yogin may eat while practising Yoga. (28)

लघुपाकं प्रियं स्निग्धं तथा धातुप्रपोषणम् ।
मनोभिलषितं योग्यं योगी भोजनमाचरेत् ॥ २९ ॥

Easily digestible, agreeable and cooling foods which nourish the elements of the body, a Yogin may eat according to his desire. (29)

कठिनं दुरितं पूतिमुष्णं पर्युषितं तथा ।
अतिशीतं चातिचोष्णं भक्ष्यं योगी विवर्जयेत् ॥ ३० ॥

But a Yogin should avoid hard (not easily digestible), sinful, or putrid, very hot, or very stale, as well as very cooling or very much exciting food. (30)

प्रात:स्नानोपवासादि कायक्लेशविधिं तथा ।
एकाहारं निराहारं यामान्ते च न कारयेत् ॥ ३१ ॥

He should avoid early (morning, before sunrise) baths, fasting, etc., or anything giving pain to the body ; so also is prohibited to him eating only once a day, or not eating at all. But he may remain without food for 3 hours. (31)

एवं विधिविधानेन प्राणायामं समाचरेत् ।
आरम्भे प्रथमे कुर्यात्क्षीराज्यं नित्यभोजनम् ।
मध्याह्ने चैव सायाह्ने भोजनद्वयमाचरेत् ॥ ३२ ॥

Regulating his life in this way, let him practise Prāṇāyāma. In the beginning before commencing it, he should take a little milk and ghee daily, and take his food twice daily, once at noon, and once in the evening. (32)

इति मिताहार: ।

अथ नाडीशुद्धिः ।

कुशासने मृगाजिने व्याघ्राजिने च कम्बले ।
स्थलासने समासीनः प्राङ्मुखो वाऽप्युदङ्मुखः ।
नाडीशुद्धिं समासाद्य प्राणायामं समभ्यसेत् ॥ ३३ ॥

4. PURIFICATION OF NĀḌIS

He should sit on a seat of Kuś́a-grass, or on antelope skin, or tiger skin or a blanket, or on earth, calmly and quietly, facing east or north. Having purified the nāḍīs, let him begin Prāṇāyāma. (33)

चण्डकापालिरुवाच ।

नाडीशुद्धिं कथं कुर्यान्नाडीशुद्धिस्तु कीदृशी ।
तत्सर्वं श्रोतुमिच्छामि तद्वदस्व दयानिधे ॥ ३४ ॥

CAṆḌAKĀPĀLI SAID

Ocean of mercy! How are nāḍīs purified, what is the purification of nāḍīs; I want to learn all this; recite this to me. (34)

घेरण्ड उवाच—

मलाकुलासु नाडीषु मारुतो नैव गच्छति ।
प्राणायामः कथं सिध्येत्तत्त्वज्ञानं कथं भवेत् ।
तस्मान्नाडीशुद्धिमादौ प्राणायामं ततोऽभ्यसेत् ॥ ३५ ॥

GHERAṆḌA SAID

The Vāyu does not (cannot) enter the nāḍīs so long as they are full of impurities (*e.g.*, fæces, etc.). How then can Prāṇāyāma be accomplished? How can there be knowledge of Tattvas? Therefore, first the Nāḍīs should be purified, and then Prāṇāyāma should be practised. (35)

नाडीशुद्धिर्द्विधा प्रोक्ता समनुर्निर्मनुस्तथा ।
बीजेन समनुं कुर्यान्निर्मनुं धौतिकर्मणा ॥ ३६ ॥

The purification of nāḍīs is of two sorts: Samanu and Nirmanu. The Samanu is done by a mental process with Bīja-mantra. The Nirmanu is performed by physical cleanings. (36)

धौतिकर्म पुरा प्रोक्तं षट्कर्मसाधने यथा ।
शृणुष्व समनुं चण्ड नाडीशुद्धिर्यथा भवेत् ॥ ३७ ॥

The physical cleanings or Dhautis have already been taught. They consist of the six Sādhanas. Now, O Caṇḍa, listen to the Samanu process of purifying the vessels. (37)

उपविश्यासने योगी पद्मासनं समाचरेत् ।
गुर्वादिन्यासनं कुर्याद्यथैव गुरुभाषितम् ।
नाडीशुद्धिं प्रकुर्वीत प्राणायामविशुद्धये ॥ ३८ ॥

Sitting in the Padmâsana posture, and performing the adoration of the Guru, etc., as taught by the Teacher, let him perform purification of Nâḍīs for success in Prâṇâyâma. (38)

वायुबीजं ततो ध्यात्वा धूम्रवर्णं सतेजसम् ।
चन्द्रेण पूरयेद्वायुं बीजं षोडशकैः सुधीः ॥ ३९ ॥
चतुःषष्ट्या मात्रया च कुम्भकेनैव धारयेत् ।
द्वात्रिंशन्मात्रया वायुं सूर्यनाड्या च रेचयेत् ॥ ४० ॥

Contemplating on Vâyu-Bīja (*i.e.*, यं), full of energy and of a smoke-colour, let him draw in breath by the left nostril, repeating the Bīja sixteen times. This is Pūraka. Let him restrain the breath for a period of sixty-four repetitions of the Mantra. This is Kumbhaka. Then let him expel the air by the right nostril slowly during a period occupied by repeating the Mantra thirty-two times. (39—40)

उत्थाप्याग्निं नाभिमूलाद् ध्यायेत्तेजोऽवनीयुतम् ।
वह्निबीजषोडशेन सूर्यनाड्या च पूरयेत् ॥ ४१ ॥
चतुःषष्ट्या मात्रया च कुम्भकेनैव धारयेत् ।
द्वात्रिंशन्मात्रया वायुं शशिनाड्या च रेचयेत् ॥ ४२ ॥

The root of the navel is the seat of Agni-Tattva. Raising the fire from that place, join the Pṛthivī-Tattva with it; then contemplate on this mixed light. Then repeating sixteen times the Agni-Bīja (रं), let him draw in breath by the right nostril, and retain it for the period of sixty-four repetitions of the Mantra, and then expel it by the left nostril for a period of thirty-two repetitions of the Mantra. (41—42)

नासाग्रे शशधृग्बिम्बं ध्यात्वा ज्योत्स्नासमन्वितम् ।
ठं बीजं षोडशेनैव इडया पूरयेन्मरुत् ॥ ४३ ॥
चतुःषष्ट्या मात्रया च वं बीजेनैव धारयेत् ।
अमृतं प्लावितं ध्यात्वा नाडीधौतिं विभावयेत् ।
द्वात्रिंशेन लकारेण दृढं भाव्यं विरेचयेत् ॥ ४४ ॥

Then fixing the gaze on the tip of the nose and contemplating the luminous reflection of the moon there, let him inhale through the left nostril, repeating the Bīja ṭhaṃ (ठं) sixteen times; let him retain it by repeating the Bīja (ठं) sixty-four times; in the meanwhile imagine (or contemplate) that the nectar flowing from the moon at the tip of the nose runs through all the vessels of the body, and purifies them. Thus contemplating, let him exhale repeating thirty-two times the Pṛthivī Bīja laṃ (लं). (43—44)

एवंविधां नाडीशुद्धिं कृत्वा नाडीं विशोधयेत् ।
दृढो भूत्वाऽऽसनं कृत्वा प्राणायामं समाचरेत् ॥ ४५ ॥

By these three Prāṇāyāmas the nāḍīs are purified. Then sitting firmly in a posture, let him begin regular Prāṇāyāma. (45)

कुम्भकभेदाः ।

सहितः सूर्यभेदश्च उज्जायी शीतली तथा ।
भस्त्रिका भ्रामरी मूर्च्छा केवली चाष्ट कुम्भकाः ॥४६॥

KINDS OF KUMBHAKA

The Kumbhakas or retentions of breath are of eight sorts; Sahita, Sūrya-bheda, Ujjāyī, Sītalī, Bhastrikā, Bhrāmarī, Mūrcchā and Kevalī. (46)

सहितो द्विविधः प्रोक्तः सगर्भश्च निगर्भकः ।
सगर्भो बीजमुच्चार्य निगर्भो बीजवर्जितः ॥ ४७ ॥

1. SAHITA

The Sahita Kumbhaka is of two sorts: Sagarbha and Nigarbha. The Kumbhaka performed by the repetition of Bīja Mantra is Sagarbha; that done without such repetition is Nigarbha. (47)

प्राणायामं सगर्भं च प्रथमं कथयामि ते ।
सुखासने चोपविश्य प्राङ्मुखो वाऽप्युदङ्मुखः ।
रजोगुणं विधिं ध्यायेद्रक्तवर्णमवर्णकम् ॥ ४८ ॥

First I shall tell thee the Sagarbha Prāṇāyāma. Sitting in Sukhāsana posture, facing east or north, let one contemplate on Brahmā full of Rajas quality of a blood-red colour, in the form of the letter अ. (48)

इडया पूरयेद्वायुं मात्रया षोडशैः सुधीः ।
पूरकान्ते कुम्भकाद्ये कर्तव्यस्तूड्डियानकः ॥ ४९ ॥

Let the wise practitioner inhale by the left nostril, repeating अ sixteen times. Then before he begins retention (but at the end of inhalation), let him perform Uḍḍīyānabandha. (49)

सत्त्वमयं हरिं ध्यात्वा उकारं कृष्णवर्णकम् ।
चतुःषष्ट्या च मात्रया कुम्भकेनैव धारयेत् ॥ ५० ॥

Then let him retain breath by repeating उ sixty-four times, contemplating on Hari, of a black colour and Sattva quality. (50)

तमोमयं शिवं ध्यात्वा मकारं शुक्लवर्णकम् ।
द्वात्रिंशन्मात्रया चैव रेचयेद्विधिना पुनः ॥ ५१ ॥

Then let him exhale the breath through the right nostril by repeating makāra (म) thirty-two times, contemplating S'iva of a white colour and of Tamas quality. (51)

पुनः पिङ्गलयाऽऽपूर्य कुम्भकेनैव धारयेत् ।
इडया रेचयेत्पश्चात् तद्बीजेन क्रमेण तु ॥ ५२ ॥

Then again inhale through Piṅgalā (right nostril), retain by Kumbhaka, and exhale by Iḍā (left), in the method taught above, changing the nostrils alternately. (52)

अनुलोमविलोमेन वारं वारं च साधयेत् ।
पूरकान्ते कुम्भकान्तं धृतनासापुटद्वयम् ।
कनिष्ठानामिकाङ्गुष्ठैस्तर्जनीमध्यमे विना ॥ ५३ ॥

Let him practise, thus alternating the nostrils again and again. When inhalation is completed, close both nostrils, the right one by the thumb and the left one by the ring-finger and little-finger, never using the index and middle-fingers. The nostrils to be closed so long as Kumbhaka is. (53)

प्राणायामो निगर्भस्तु विना बीजेन जायते ।
वामजानूपरिन्यस्तवामपाणितलं भ्रमेत् ।
एकादिशतपर्यन्तं पूरकुम्भकरेचकम् ॥ ५४ ॥

The Nigarbha (or simple or mantraless) Prāṇāyāma is performed without the repetition of Bīja mantra; and the period of Pūraka (inhalation or inspiration), Kumbhaka (retention), and Recaka (expiration), may be extended from one to hundred mātrās. (54)

उत्तमा विंशतिर्मात्रा षोडशी मात्रा मध्यमा ।
अधमा द्वादशी मात्रा प्राणायामास्त्रिधा स्मृताः ॥५५॥

The best is twenty Mātrās: *i.e.*, Pūraka 20 seconds, Kumbhaka 80, and Recaka 40 seconds. The sixteen mātrās is middling, *i.e.*, 16, 64 and 32. The twelve mātras is the lowest, *i.e.*, 12, 48, 24. Thus the Prāṇāyāma is of three sorts. (55)

अधमाज्जायते धर्मो मेरुकम्पश्च मध्यमात् ।
उत्तमाच्च भूमित्यागस्त्रिविधं सिद्धिलक्षणम् ॥ ५६ ॥

By practising the lowest Prāṇāyāma for sometime, the body begins to perspire copiously; by practising the middling, the body begins to quiver (especially, there is a feeling of quivering along the spinal cord). By the highest Prāṇāyāma, one leaves the ground, *i.e.*, there is levitation. These signs attend the success of these three sorts of Prāṇāyāma. (56)

प्राणायामात्खेचरत्वं प्राणायामाद्रुजां हतिः ।
प्राणायामाच्छक्तिबोधः प्राणायामान्मनोन्मनी ।
आनन्दो जायते चित्ते प्राणायामी सुखी भवेत् ॥५७॥

By Prāṇāyāma is attained the power of levitation (Khecarī S'akti), by Prāṇāyāma diseases are cured, by Prāṇāyāma the S'akti (spiritual energy) is awakened, by Prāṇāyāma is obtained the calmness of mind and exaltation of mental powers (clairvoyance, etc.); by this, mind becomes full of bliss; verily the practitioner of Prāṇāyāma is happy. (57)

अथ सूर्यभेदकुम्भकः ।

घेरण्ड उवाच—

कथितं सहितं कुम्भं सूर्यभेदनकं शृणु ।
पूरयेत्सूर्यनाड्या च यथाशक्ति बहिर्मरुत् ॥ ५८ ॥
धारयेद् बहुयत्नेन कुम्भकेन जलन्धरैः ।
यावत्स्वेदं नखकेशाभ्यां तावत्कुर्वन्तु कुम्भकम् ॥५९॥

2. SŪRYABHEDA KUMBHAKA

GHERAṆḌA SAID

I have told thee the Sahita Kumbhaka; now hear the Sūryabheda. Inspire with all your strength the external air through the sun-tube (right nostril): retain this air with the greatest care, performing the Jālandhara Mudrā. Let the Kumbhaka be kept up until the perspiration bursts out from the tips of the nails and the roots of the hair. (58—59)

प्राणोऽपानः समानश्चोदानव्यानौ तथैव च ।
नागः कूर्मश्च कृकरो देवदत्तो धनंजयः ॥ ६० ॥

THE VĀYUS

The Vâyus are ten, namely, Prāṇa, Apāna, Samāna, Udāna and Vyāna; Nāga, Kūrma, Kṛkara, Devadatta and Dhanaṁjaya. (60)

हृदि प्राणो वहेन्नित्यमपानो गुदमण्डले ।
समानो नाभिदेशे तु उदानः कण्ठमध्यगः ॥ ६१ ॥
व्यानो व्याप्य शरीरे तु प्रधानाः पञ्च वायवः ।
प्राणाद्याः पञ्च विख्याता नागाद्याः पञ्च वायवः ॥ ६२ ॥

Their Seats

The Prāṇa moves always in the heart; the Apāna in the sphere of anus; the Samāna in the navel region; the Udāna in the throat; and the Vyāna pervades the whole body. These are the five principal Vâyus, known as Prāṇādi. They belong to the Inner body. The Nāgādi five Vâyus belong to the Outer body. (61—62)

तेषामपि च पञ्चानां स्थानानि च वदाम्यहम् ।
उद्गारे नाग आख्यातः कूर्मस्तून्मीलने स्मृतः ॥ ६३ ॥

कृकरः क्षुत्कृते ज्ञेयो देवदत्तो विजृम्भणे ।
न जहाति मृतं वाऽपि सर्वव्यापी धनंजयः ॥ ६४ ॥

I now tell thee the seats of these five
external Vâyus. The Nâga-Vâyu performs
the function of belching; the Kûrma opens
the eye-lids; the Kṛkara causes sneezing; the
Devadatta does yawning; the Dhanaṃjaya
pervades the whole gross body, and does not
leave it even after death. (63—64)

नागो गृह्णाति चैतन्यं कूर्मश्चैव निमेषणम् ।
क्षुत्तृषं कृकरश्चैव चतुर्थेन तु जृम्भणम् ।
भवेद्धनंजयाच्छब्दः क्षणमात्रं न निःसरेत् ॥ ६५ ॥

The Nâga-Vâyu gives rise to consciousness,
the Kûrma causes vision, the Kṛkara hunger
and thirst, the Devadatta produces yawning
and by Dhanaṃjaya sound is produced; this
does not leave the body even for a minute. (65)

सर्वे ते सूर्यसंभिन्ना नाभिमूलात्समुद्धरेत् ।
इडया रेचयेत्पश्चाद् धैर्येणाखण्डवेगतः ॥ ६६ ॥
पुनः सूर्येण चाकृष्य कुम्भयित्वा यथाविधि ।
रेचयित्वा साधयेत्तु क्रमेण च पुनः पुनः ॥ ६७ ॥

Let him raise all these Vāyus, which are separated by the Sūryanāḍī, from the root of the navel; then exhale by the Iḍā-nāḍī, slowly with confidence and with unbroken, continuous force. Let him again inhale through the right nostril, retaining it, as taught above, and exhale it again. Let him do this again and again. [In this process, the air is always inspired through the Sūrya-nāḍī. (66—67)]

कुम्भकः सूर्यभेदस्तु जरामृत्युविनाशकः ।
बोधयेत्कुण्डलीं शक्तिं देहाग्निं च विवर्धयेत् ।
इति ते कथितं चण्ड सूर्यभेदनमुत्तमम् ॥ ६८ ॥

Its benefits

The Sūrya-bheda Kumbhaka destroys decay and death, awakens the Kuṇḍalī s'akti, increases the bodily fire. O Caṇḍa! thus have I taught thee the Sūryabhedana Kumbhaka. (68)

N.B.—The description of this process, as given in Haṭha-Yoga Pradīpikā, is somewhat different. It says: Soon after Pūraka (inspiration), one should perform Jālandhara and at the end of Kumbhaka, but before Recaka perform the Uḍḍīyānabandha. Then quickly contract the anal orifice by Mūlabandha, contract the throat, pull in the stomach towards the back; by this process the air is forced into the Brahma-nāḍī (Suṣumṇā). Raise the Apāna up, lower the Prāṇa, below the Kanda; a Yogin becomes free from decay: the air should be drawn through the right nostril and expelled through the left.

अथ उज्जायी कुम्भकः ।

नासाभ्यां वायुमाकृष्य मुखमध्ये च धारयेत् ।
हृद्गलाभ्यां समाकृष्य वायुं वक्त्रे च धारयेत् ॥ ६९ ॥

3. UJJĀYĪ

Close the mouth, draw in the external air by both the nostrils, and pull the internal air from the lungs and throat; retain them in the mouth. (69)

मुखं प्रक्षाल्य संवन्ध कुर्याज्जालन्धरं ततः ।
आशक्ति कुम्भकं कृत्वा धारयेदविरोधतः ॥ ७० ॥

Then having washed the mouth (*i.e.*, expelled the air through mouth) perform Jālandhara. Let him perform Kumbhaka with all his might and retain the air unhindered. (70)

उज्जायीकुम्भकं कृत्वा सर्वकार्याणि साधयेत् ।
न भवेत्कफरोगश्च क्रूरवायुरजीर्णकम् ॥ ७१ ॥

आमवातः क्षयः कासो ज्वरः प्लीहा न विद्यते ।
जरामृत्युविनाशाय चोज्जायीं साधयेन्नरः ॥ ७२ ॥

All works are accomplished by Ujjāyī Kumbhaka. He is never attacked by phlegm-diseases, or nerve-diseases, or indigestion, or dysentery, or consumption, or cough; or fever or [enlarged] spleen. Let a man perform Ujjāyī to destroy decay and death. (71—72)

N.B.—See the Haṭha-Yoga Pradīpikā, Chap. II, 51, 53, for a different description of this.

अथ शीतलीकुम्भकः ।

जिह्वया वायुमाकृष्य चोदरे पूरयेच्छनैः ।
क्षणं च कुम्भकं कृत्वा नासाभ्यां रेचयेत्पुनः ॥ ७३ ॥

4. SĪTALĪ

Draw in the air through the mouth (with the lips contracted and tongue thrown out), and fill the stomach slowly. Retain it there for a short time. Then exhale it through both the nostrils. (73)

सर्वदा साधयेद्योगी शीतलीकुम्भकं शुभम् ।
अजीर्णं कफपित्तं च नैव तस्य प्रजायते ॥ ७४ ॥

Let the Yogin always practise this S'ītalī Kumbhaka, giver of bliss; by so doing, he will be free from indigestion, phlegm and bilious disorders. (74)

अथ भस्त्रिकाकुम्भकः ।

भस्त्रिका लोहकाराणां यथा क्रमेण संभ्रमेत् ।
तथा वायुं च नासाभ्यामुभाभ्यां चालयेच्छनैः ॥७५॥

5. BHASTRIKĀ (BELLOW)

As the bellows of the ironsmith constantly dilate and contract, similarly let him slowly draw in the air by both the nostrils and expand the stomach; then throw it out quickly (the wind making sound like bellows). (75)

एवं विंशतिवारं च कृत्वा कुर्याच्च कुम्भकम् ।
तदन्ते चालयेद्वायुं पूर्वोक्तं च यथाविधि ॥ ७६ ॥
त्रिवारं साधयेदेनं भस्त्रिकाकुम्भकं सुधीः ।
न च रोगो न च क्लेश आरोग्यं च दिने दिने ॥७७॥

Having thus inspired and expired quickly twenty times, let him perform Kumbhaka; then let him expel it by the previous method. Let the wise one perform this Bhastrikā (bellows-like) Kumbhaka thrice: he will never suffer from any disease and will be always healthy. (76—77)

अथ भ्रामरीकुम्भकः ।

अर्धरात्रे गते योगी जन्तूनां शब्दवर्जिते ।
कर्णौ पिधाय हस्ताभ्यां कुर्यात्पूरककुम्भकम् ॥ ७८ ॥

6. BHRĀMARĪ (OR BEETLE-DRONING KUMBHAKA)

At past midnight, in a place where there are no sounds of any animals, etc., to be heard, let the Yogin practise Pūraka and Kumbhaka, closing the ears by the hands. (78)

शृणुयाद्दक्षिणे कर्णे नादमन्तर्गतं शुभम् ।
प्रथमं झिल्लिकानादं वंशीनादं ततः परम् ॥ ७९ ॥
मेघझर्झरभ्रमरी घण्टा कास्यं ततः परम् ।
तुरीभेरीमृदङ्गादिनिनादानकदुन्दुभिः ॥ ८० ॥

He will hear then various internal sounds in his right ear. The first sound will be like that of crickets, then that of a flute, then that of a thunder, then that of a drum, then that of a beetle, then that of bells, then those of gongs of bell-metal, trumpets, kettle-drums, mṛdaṅga, military drums, and dundubhi, etc. (79—80)

एवं नानाविधो नादो जायते नित्यमभ्यसात् ।
अनाहतस्य शब्दस्य तस्य शब्दस्य यो ध्वनिः ॥८१॥
ध्वनेरन्तर्गतं ज्योतिर्ज्योतिरन्तर्गतं मनः ।
तन्मनो विलयं याति तद्विष्णोः परमं पदम् ।
एवं भ्रामरीसंसिद्धिः समाधिसिद्धिमाप्नुयात् ॥ ८२ ॥

Thus various sounds are cognised by daily practice of this Kumbhaka. Last of all is heard the Anâhata sound rising from the heart; of this sound there is a resonance, in that resonance there is a Light. In that Light the mind should be immersed. When the mind is absorbed, then it reaches the Highest seat of Viṣṇu (parama-pada). By success in this Bhrâmarī Kumbhaka one gets success in Samâdhi. (81—82)

अथ मूर्च्छाकुम्भकः ।

सुखेन कुम्भकं कृत्वा मनश्च भ्रुवोरन्तरम् ।
संत्यज्य विषयान्सर्वान्मनोमूर्च्छा सुखप्रदा ।
आत्मनि मनसो योगादानन्दो जायते ध्रुवम् ॥ ८३ ॥

7. MŪRCCHĀ

Having performed Kumbhaka with comfort, let him withdraw the mind from all objects and fix it in the space between the eyebrows. This causes fainting of the mind, and gives happiness. For, by thus joining the Manas with the Ātman, the bliss of Yoga is certainly obtained. (83)

अथ केवलीकुम्भकः ।

हंकारेण बहिर्याति सःकारेण विशेत्पुनः ।
षट्शतानि दिवारात्रौ सहस्राण्येकविंशतिः ।
अजपां नाम गायत्रीं जीवो जपति सर्वदा ॥ ८४ ॥

8. KEVALĪ

The breath of every person in entering makes the sound of "saḥ" and in coming out, that of "ham". These two sounds make सोऽहम् (so'ham "I am He") or हंस: (haṃsaḥ "The Great Swan"). Throughout a day and a night there are twenty-one thousand and six hundred such respirations, (that is, 15 respirations per minute). Every living being (Jīva) performs this japa unconsciously, but constantly. This is called Ajapā gāyattrī. (84)

मूलाधारे यथा हंसस्तथा हि हृदि पङ्कजे ।
तथा नासापुटद्वन्द्वे त्रिभिर्हंससमागमः ॥ ८५ ॥

This Ajapā-japa is performed in three places, *i.e.*, in the Mūlādhāra (the space between the anus and membranum virile), in the Anāhata lotus (heart) and in the Ājñā lotus (the space where the nostrils unite). (85)

षण्णवत्यङ्गुलीमानं शरीरं कर्मरूपकम् ।
देहाद्बहिर्गतो वायुः स्वभावाद्द्वादशाङ्गुलिः ॥ ८६ ॥
गायने षोडशाङ्गुल्यो भोजने विंशतिस्तथा ।
चतुर्विंशाङ्गुलिः पन्थे निद्रायां त्रिंशदङ्गुलिः ।
मैथुने षट्त्रिंशदुक्तं व्यायामे च ततोऽधिकम् ॥ ८७ ॥

This body is ninety-six digits long (*i.e.*, six feet) as a standard. The ordinary length of the air-current when expired is twelve digits (nine inches); in singing, its length becomes sixteen digits (one foot); in eating, it is twenty digits (15 inches); in walking, it is twenty-four digits (18 inches); in sleep, it is thirty digits ($22\frac{1}{2}$ inches); in copulation.

it is thirty-six digits (27 inches), and in taking physical exercise, it is more than that. (86—87)

स्वभावेऽस्य गतेर्न्यूने परमायुः प्रवर्धते ।
आयुःक्षयोऽधिके प्रोक्तो मारुते चान्तराद्गते ॥ ८८ ॥

By decreasing the natural length of the expired current from nine inches to less and less, there takes place increase of life; and by increasing the current, there is decrease of life. (88)

तस्मात्प्राणे स्थिते देहे मरणं नैव जायते ।
वायुना घटसंबन्धे भवेत्केवलकुम्भकम् ॥ ८९ ॥

So long as breath remains in the body there is no death. When the full length of the wind is all confined in the body, nothing being allowed to go out, it is Kevala Kumbhaka. (89)

यावज्जीवं जपेन्मन्त्रमजपासंख्यकेवलम् ।
अद्यावधि धृतं संख्याविभ्रमं केवलीकृते ॥ ९० ॥
अत एव हि कर्तव्यः केवलीकुम्भको नरैः ।
केवली चाजपासंख्या द्विगुणा च मनोन्मनी ॥ ९१ ॥

All Jīvas are constantly and unconsciously reciting this Ajapā Mantra, only for a fixed number of times every day. But a Yogin should recite this consciously and counting the numbers. By doubling the number of Ajapā (*i.e.*, by 30 respirations per minute), the state of Manonmanī (fixedness of mind) is attained. There are no regular Recaka and Pūraka in this process. It is only (Kevala) Kumbhaka. (90—91)

नासाभ्यां वायुमाकृष्य केवलं कुम्भकं चरेत् ।
एकादिकचतुःषष्टिं धारयेत्प्रथमे दिने ॥ ९२ ॥

By inspiring air by both nostrils, let him perform Kevala Kumbhaka. On the first day, let him retain breath from one to sixty-four times. (92)

केवलीमष्टधा कुर्याद्यामे यामे दिने दिने ।
अथ वा पञ्चधा कुर्याद्यथा तत्कथयामि ते ॥ ९३ ॥
प्रातर्मध्याह्नसायाह्ने मध्येरात्रि चतुर्थके ।
त्रिसंध्यमथ वा कुर्यात्सममाने दिने दिने ॥ ९४ ॥

This Kevalī should be performed eight times a day, once every three hours; or one may do it five times a day, as I shall tell thee. First in the early morning, then at noon, then in the twilight, then at midnight, and then in the fourth quarter of the night. Or one may do it thrice a day, *i.e.*, in the morning, noon and evening. (93—94)

पञ्चवारं दिने वृद्धिर्वारैकं च दिने तथा ।
अजपापरिमाणं च यावत्सिद्धिः प्रजायते ॥ ९५ ॥
प्राणायामं केवली च तदा वदति योगवित् ।
केवलीकुम्भके सिद्धे किं न सिध्यति भूतले ॥ ९६ ॥

इति श्रीघेरण्डसंहितायां घेरण्डचण्डसंवादे घटस्थयोगप्रकरणे प्राणायामप्रयोगो नाम पञ्चमोपदेशः ।

So long as success is not obtained in Kevalī, he should increase the length of Ajapā japa every day, one to five times. He who knows Prāṇāyāma and Kevalī is the real Yogin. What can he not accomplish in this world who has acquired success in Kevalī Kumbhaka? (95—96)

End of the fifth lesson

षष्ठोपदेशः

LESSON THE SIXTH

अथ ध्यानयोगः ।

घेरण्ड उवाच —

स्थूलं ज्योतिस्तथा सूक्ष्मं ध्यानस्य त्रिविधं विदुः ।
स्थूलं मूर्तिमयं प्रोक्तं ज्योतिस्तेजोमयं तथा ।
सूक्ष्मं बिन्दुमयं ब्रह्म कुण्डली परदेवता ॥ १ ॥

DHYĀNA-YOGA

GHERAṆḌA SAID

The Dhyāna or contemplation is of three sorts: gross, luminous and subtle. When a particular figure, (such as one's Guru or Deity) is contemplated on, it is Sthūla or gross contemplation. When Brahman or Prakṛti is contemplated on as a mass of light, it is called Jyotis-contemplation. When Brahman as Bindu (point) and Kuṇḍalī force is contemplated on, it is Sūkṣma or Subtle contemplation. (1)

अथ स्थूलध्यानम् ।

स्वकायहृदये ध्यायेत्सुधासागरमुत्तमम् ।
तन्मध्ये रत्नद्वीपं तु सुरत्नवालुकामयम् ॥ २ ॥
चतुर्दिक्षु नीपतरुं बहुपुष्पसमन्वितम् ।
नीपोपवनसंकुलैर्वेष्टितं परिखा इव ॥ ३ ॥
मालतीमल्लिकाजातीकेसरैश्चम्पकैस्तथा ।
पारिजातैः स्थलपद्मैर्गन्धामोदितदिङ्मुखैः ॥ ४ ॥
तन्मध्ये संस्मरेद्योगी कल्पवृक्षं मनोहरम् ।
चतुःशाखाचतुर्वेदं नित्यपुष्पफलान्वितम् ॥ ५ ॥
भ्रमराः कोकिलास्तत्र गुञ्जन्ति निगदन्ति च ।
ध्यायेत्तत्र स्थिरो भूत्वा महामाणिक्यमण्डपम् ॥ ६ ॥
तन्मध्ये तु स्मरेद्योगी पर्यङ्कं सुमनोहरम् ।
तत्रेष्टदेवतां ध्यायेद्यद्ध्यानं गुरुभाषितम् ॥ ७ ॥
यस्य देवस्य यद्रूपं यथा भूषणवाहनम् ।
तद्रूपं ध्यायते नित्यं स्थूलध्यानमिदं विदुः ॥ ८ ॥

1. Sthūla Dhyāna

(Having closed the eyes), let him contemplate that there is a sea of nectar in the region of his heart: that in the midst of that sea an island of precious stones, the very sand of which is pulverised diamonds and rubies. That on all sides of it, Kadamba trees, laden with sweet flowers; that, next to those trees, like a rampart, a row of flowering trees, such as mālatī, mallikā, jātī, kesara, campaka, pārijāta and padma, and that the fragrance of these flowers is spread all round, in every quarter. In the middle of this garden, let the Yogin imagine that there stands a beautiful Kalpa tree, having four branches, representing the four Vedas, and that it is full of flowers and fruits. Beetles are humming there and cuckoos singing. Beneath that tree, let him imagine a rich platform of precious gems, and on that a costly throne inlaid with jewels, and that on that throne sits his particular Deity, as taught to him by his Guru. Let him contemplate on the appropriate form, ornaments and vehicle of that Deity. The constant contemplation of such a form is Sthūla Dhyāna. (2—8)

प्रकारान्तरम् ।

सहस्रारे महापद्मे कर्णिकायां विचिन्तयेत् ।
विलग्नसहितं पद्मं दलैर्द्वादशभिर्युतम् ॥ ९ ॥

शुक्लवर्णं महातेजो द्वादशैर्बीजभाषितम् ।
हसक्षमलवरयुं हसखफ्रें यथाक्रमम् ॥ १० ॥
तन्मध्ये कर्णिकायां तु अकथादिरेखात्रयम् ।
हळक्षकोणसंयुक्तं प्रणवं तत्र वर्तते ॥ ११ ॥

ANOTHER PROCESS

Let the Yogin imagine that in the pericarp of the great thousand-petalled Lotus (Brain) there is a smaller lotus having twelve petals. Its colour is white, highly luminous, having twelve bīja letters, named ह, स, क्ष, म, ल, व, र, युं, ह, स, ख, फ्रें, (ha, sa, kṣa, ma, la, va, ra, yuṁ, ha, sa, kha, phreṃ). In the pericarp of this smaller lotus there are three lines forming a triangle अ, क, थ (a, ka, tha): having three angles called ह, ळ, क्ष (ha, ḷa, kṣa): and in the middle of this triangle, there is the Praṇava ओम् Om. (9—11)

नादबिन्दुमयं पीठं ध्यायेत्तत्र मनोहरम् ।
तत्रोपरि हंसयुग्मं पादुका तत्र वर्तते ॥ १२ ॥

Then let him contemplate that in that there is a beautiful seat having Nāda and Bindu.

On that seat there are two swans, and a pair of wooden sandals. (12)

ध्यायेत्तत्र गुरुं देवं द्विभुजं च त्रिलोचनम् ।
श्वेताम्बरधरं देवं शुक्लगन्धानुलेपनम् ॥ १३ ॥
शुक्लपुष्पमयं माल्यं रक्तशक्तिसमन्वितम् ।
एवंविधगुरुध्यानात्स्थूलध्यानं प्रसिध्यति ॥ १४ ॥

There let him contemplate his Guru Deva, having two arms and three eyes, and dressed in pure white, anointed with white sandal-paste, wearing garlands of white flowers; to the left of whom stands Śakti of blood-red colour. By thus contemplating the Guru, the Sthūla Dhyāna is attained. (13—14)

अथ ज्योतिर्ध्यानम् ।

घेरण्ड उवाच—

स्थूलध्यानं तु कथितं तेजोध्यानं शृणुष्व मे ।
यद्ध्यानेन योगसिद्धिरात्मप्रत्यक्षमेव च ॥ १५ ॥

2. JYOTIRDHYĀNA

GHERAṆḌA SAID

I have told thee the Sthūla Dhyāna; listen now to the contemplation of Light, by which the Yogin attains success and sees his Self. (15)

मूलाधारे कुण्डलिनी भुजगाकाररूपिणी ।
तत्र तिष्ठति जीवात्मा प्रदीपकलिकाकृतिः ।
ध्यायेत्तेजोमयं ब्रह्म तेजोध्यानं परात्परम् ॥ १६ ॥

In the Mūlādhāra is kuṇḍalinī of the form of a serpent. The Jīvātman is there like the flame of a lamp. Contemplate on this flame as the Luminous Brahman. This is the Tejodhyāna or Jyotirdhyāna. (16)

प्रकारान्तरम् ।

भ्रुवोर्मध्ये मनऊर्ध्वे यत्तेजः प्रणवात्मकम् ।
ध्यायेज्ज्वालावलीयुक्तं तेजोध्यानं तदेव हि ॥ १७ ॥

ANOTHER PROCESS

In the middle of the eye-brows, above the Manas, there is the Light of Om. Let him contemplate on this flame. This is another method of contemplation of Light. (17)

अथ सूक्ष्मध्यानम् ।

घेरण्ड उवाच—

तेजोध्यानं श्रुतं चण्ड सूक्ष्मध्यानं शृणुष्व मे ।
बहुभाग्यवशाद्यस्य कुण्डली जाग्रती भवेत् ॥ १८ ॥

आत्मना सह योगेन नेत्ररन्ध्राद्विनिर्गता ।
विहरेद्राजमार्गे च चञ्चलत्वान्न दृश्यते ॥ १९ ॥

3. SŪKṢMA DHYĀNA

GHERAṆḌA SAID

O Caṇḍa! thou hast heard the Tejodhyāna, listen now to the Sūkṣma Dhyāna. When by a great good fortune, the kuṇḍalī is awakened, it joins with the Ātman and leaves the body through the portals of the eyes: and enjoys itself by walking in the royal road. It cannot be seen on account of its subtleness and great changeability. (18—19)

शांभवीमुद्रया योगो ध्यानयोगेन सिध्यति ।
सूक्ष्मध्यानमिदं गोप्यं देवानामपि दुर्लभम् ॥ २० ॥

The Yogin, however, attains this success by performing S'āmbhavī Mudrā, *i.e.*, by gazing fixedly at space without winking. (Then he will see his Sūkṣma S'arīra.) This is called Sūkṣma Dhyāna, difficult to be attained even by the Devas, as it is a great mystery. (20)

स्थूलध्यानाच्छतगुणं तेजोध्यानं प्रचक्षते ।
तेजोध्यानाल्लक्षगुणं सूक्ष्मध्यानं परात्परम् ॥ २१ ॥

The contemplation on Light is a hundred times superior to contemplation on Form; and a hundred thousand times superior to Tejodhyāna is the contemplation on the Sūkṣma. (21)

इति ते कथितं चण्ड ध्यानयोगं सुदुर्लभम् ।
आत्मा साक्षाद्भवेद्यस्मात्तस्माद्ध्यानं विशिष्यते ॥२२॥

इति श्रीघेरण्डसंहितायां घेरण्डचण्डसंवादे घटस्थयोगे
सप्तमसाधने ध्यानयोगो नाम षष्ठोपदेशः ।

O Caṇḍa! thus have I told thee Dhyāna Yoga—a most precious knowledge; for, by it, there is direct perception of the Self. Hence Dhyāna is belauded. (22)

End of the sixth lesson

सप्तमोपदेशः ।

LESSON THE SEVENTH

अथ समाधियोगः ।

घेरण्ड उवाच—

समाधिश्च परो योगो बहुभाग्येन लभ्यते ।
गुरोः कृपाप्रसादेन प्राप्यते गुरुभक्तितः ॥ १ ॥

SAMĀDHI YOGA

GHERAṆḌA SAID

The Samādhi is a great Yoga; it is acquired by great good fortune. It is obtained through the grace and kindness of the Guru, and by intense devotion to him. (1)

विद्याप्रतीतिः स्वगुरुप्रतीतिरात्मप्रतीतिर्मनसः प्रबोधः ।
दिने दिने यस्य भवेत्स योगी सुशोभनाभ्यासमुपैति सद्यः ॥

That Yogin quickly attains this most beautiful practice of Samâdhi, who has confidence (or faith) in knowledge, faith in his own Guru, faith in his own Self; and whose mind (manas) awakens to intelligence from day to day. (2)

घटाद्भिन्नं मनः कृत्वा चैक्यं कुर्यात्परात्मनि ।
समाधिं तं विजानीयान्मुक्तसंज्ञो दशादिभिः ॥ ३ ॥

Separate the Manas from the body, and unite it with the Paramâtman. This is known as Samâdhi or Mukti, liberation from all states of consciousness. (3)

अहं ब्रह्म न चान्योऽस्मि ब्रह्मैवाहं न शोकभाक् ।
सच्चिदानन्दरूपोऽहं नित्यमुक्तः स्वभाववान् ॥ ४ ॥

I am Brahman, I am nothing else, verily am I Brahman, I am not participator of sorrow, I am Existence, Intelligence and Bliss; always free, and one with Brahman. (4)

शांभव्या चैव खेचर्या भ्रामर्या योनिमुद्रया ।
ध्यानं नादं रसानन्दं लयसिद्धिश्चतुर्विधा ॥ ५ ॥
पञ्चधा भक्तियोगेन मनोमूर्च्छा च षड्विधा ।
षड्विधोऽयं राजयोगः प्रत्येकमवधारयेत् ॥ ६ ॥

The Samādhi is four-fold, *i.e.*, Dhyāna, Nāda, Rasānanda, and Laya respectively accomplished by S'āmbhavī Mudrā, Khecarī Mudrā, Bhrāmarī Mudrā and Yoni-Mudrā. The Bhakti-Yoga Samādhi is fifth, and Rāja-Yoga Samādhi, attained through Mano-Mūrcchā Kumbhaka, is the sixth form of Samādhi. (5—6)

अथ ध्यानयोगसमाधिः ।

शांभवीं मुद्रिकां कृत्वा आत्मप्रत्यक्षमानयेत् ।
बिन्दु ब्रह्ममयं दृष्ट्वा मनस्तत्र नियोजयेत् ॥ ७ ॥

1. Dhyāna-Yoga Samādhi

Performing the S'āmbhavī Mudrā perceive the Ātman. Having seen once the Brahman in a Bindu (point of light), fix the mind on that point. (7)

खमध्ये कुरु चात्मानमात्ममध्ये च खं कुरु ।
आत्मानं खमयं दृष्ट्वा न किंचदपि बुध्यते ।
सदाऽऽनन्दमयो भूत्वा समाधिस्थो भवेन्नरः ॥ ८ ॥

Bring the Ātman in Kha (Ether), bring the Kha (Ether or Space) in the Ātman. Thus seeing the Ātman full of Kha (Space or Brahman), nothing will obstruct him. Being full of perpetual bliss, the man enters Samādhi (Trance or Ecstasy). (8)

अथ नादयोगसमाधिः ।

खेचरीमुद्रासाधनाद् रसनोर्ध्वगता यदा ।
तदा समाधिसिद्धिः स्याद्धित्वा साधारणक्रियाम् ॥९॥

2. Nāda-Yoga Samādhi

Turn the tongue upwards, (closing the wind-passages), by performing the Khecarī Mudrā; by so doing, Samādhi (trance asphyxiation) will be induced; there is no necessity of performing anything else. (9)

अथ रसनानन्दयोगसमाधिः ।

अनिलं मन्दवेगेन भ्रामरीकुम्भकं चरेत् ।
मन्दं मन्दं रेचयेद्वायुं भृङ्गनादं ततो भवेत् ॥ १० ॥
अन्तःस्थं भ्रमरीनादं श्रुत्वा तत्र मनो नयेत् ।
समाधिर्जायते तत्र चानन्दः सोऽहमित्यतः ॥ ११ ॥

3. Rasānanda-Yoga Samādhi

Let him perform the Bhrāmarī Kumbhaka, drawing in the air slowly: expel the air slowly and slowly, when a buzzing sound like that of a beetle rises. Let him carry the Manas and place it in the centre of this sound of beetle-humming. By so doing, there will be Samādhi and by this, knowledge of *so' ham* (I am He) arises, and a great happiness takes place. (10—11)

अथ लयसिद्धियोगसमाधिः ।

योनिमुद्रां समासाद्य स्वयं शक्तिमयो भवेत् ।
सुशृङ्गाररसेनैव विहरेत्परमात्मनि ॥ १२ ॥
आनन्दमयः संभूत्वा ऐक्यं ब्रह्मणि संभवेत् ।
अहं ब्रह्मेति चाद्वैतसमाधिस्तेन जायते ॥ १३ ॥

4. LAYA-SIDDHI-YOGA SAMĀDHI

Performing the Yoni-Mudrā let him imagine that he is S'akti, and with this feeling enjoy the bliss of Paramātman (and that both have been united in one). By this he becomes full of bliss, and realises *Ahaṃ Brahma*, 'I am Brahman'. This conduces to Advaita Samādhi. (12—13)

अथ भक्तियोगसमाधिः ।

स्वकीयहृदये ध्यायेदिष्टदेवस्वरूपकम् ।
चिन्तयेद्भक्तियोगेन परमाह्लादपूर्वकम् ॥ १४ ॥

आनन्दाश्रुपुलकेन दशाभावः प्रजायते ।
समाधिः संभवेत्तेन संभवेच्च मनोन्मनी ॥ १५ ॥

5. BHAKTI-YOGA SAMĀDHI

Let him contemplate within his heart his special Deity; let him be full of ecstasy by such contemplation, let him, with thrill, shed tears of happiness, and by so doing he will become entranced. This leads to Samādhi and Manonmanī. (14—15)

अथ राजयोगसमाधिः ।

मनोमूर्च्छां समासाद्य मन आत्मनि योजयेत् ।
परात्मनः समायोगात्समाधिं समवाप्नुयात् ॥ १६ ॥

6. RĀJA-YOGA SAMĀDHI

Performing Manomūrcchā Kumbhaka, unite the Manas with the Ātman. By this Union is obtained Rāja-Yoga Samādhi. (16)

अथ समाधियोगमाहात्म्यम् ।

इति ते कथितश्चण्ड समाधिर्मुक्तिलक्षणम् ।
राजयोगसमाधिः स्यादेकात्मन्येव साधनम् ।
उन्मनी सहजावस्था सर्वे चैकात्मवाचकाः ॥ १७ ॥

7. Praise of Samādhi

O Caṇḍa! thus have I told thee about Samādhi which leads to emancipation. Rāja-Yoga Samādhi, Unmanī, Sahajāvasthā are all synonyms, and mean the Union of Manas with Ātman. (17)

जले विष्णुः स्थले विष्णुर्विष्णुः पर्वतमस्तके ।
ज्वालामालाकुले विष्णुः सर्वं विष्णुमयं जगत् ॥१८॥

Viṣṇu is in water, Viṣṇu is in the earth, Viṣṇu is on the peak of the mountain; Viṣṇu is in the midst of the volcanic fires and flames; the whole universe is full of Viṣṇu. (18)

भूचराः खेचराश्चामी यावन्तो जीवजन्तवः ।
वृक्षगुल्मलतावल्लीतृणाद्या वारि पर्वताः ।
सर्वं ब्रह्म विजानीयात्सर्वं पश्यति चात्मनि ॥ १९ ॥

All those that walk on land or move in the air, all living and animate creation, trees, shrubs, roots, creepers and grass, etc., oceans and mountains—all, know ye to be Brahman. See them all in Ātman. (19)

आत्मा घटस्थचैतन्यमद्वैतं शाश्वतं परम् ।
घटाद्विभिन्नतो ज्ञात्वा वीतरागं विवासनम् ॥ २० ॥

The Ātman confined in the body is Caitanya or Consciousness, it is without a second, the Eternal, the Highest; knowing it separate from body, let him be free from desires and passions. (20)

एवं मिथः समाधिः स्यात्सर्वसंकल्पवर्जितः ।
स्वदेहे पुत्रदारादिबान्धवेषु धनादिषु ।
सर्वेषु निर्ममो भूत्वा समाधिं समवाप्नुयात् ॥ २१ ॥

Thus is Samādhi obtained free from all desires. Free from attachment to his own body, to son, wife, friends, kinsmen, or riches; being free from all, let him obtain fully the Samādhi. (21)

तत्त्वं लयामृतं गोप्यं शिवोक्तं विविधानि च ।
तेषां संक्षेपमादाय कथितं मुक्तिलक्षणम् ॥ २२ ॥

S'iva has revealed many Tattvas, such as Laya Amṛta, etc., of them, I have told thee an abstract, leading to emancipation. (22)

इति ते कथितश्चण्ड समाधिर्दुर्लभः परः ।
यं ज्ञात्वा न पुनर्जन्म जायते भूमिमण्डले ॥ २३ ॥

इति श्रीघेरण्डसंहितायां घेरण्डचण्डसंवादे घटस्थयोगसाधने योगस्य
सप्तसारे समाधियोगो नाम सप्तमोपदेशः समाप्तः ।

O Caṇḍa ! thus have I told thee of Samādhi, difficult of attainment. By knowing this, there is no rebirth in this Sphere. (23)

End of the seventh lesson

Lightning Source UK Ltd.
Milton Keynes UK

177662UK00001B/144/P

9 781447 402374